lonely 🌐 planet

AF215340

POCKET

BRUGES &
BRUSSELS

Mélissa Monaco & Helena Smith

Contents

Plan Your Trip 4

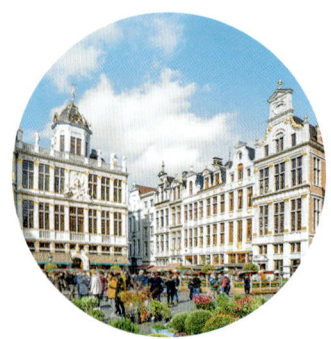

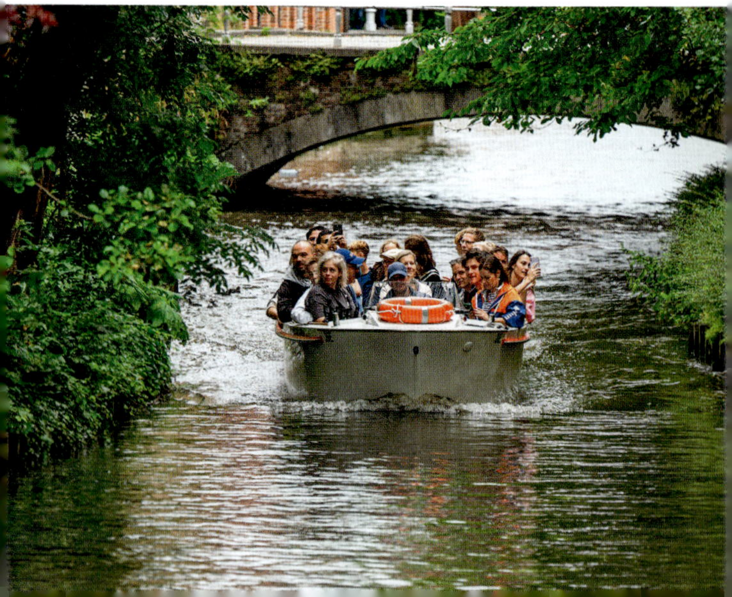

Top: Grand-Place (p84)
Bottom: Minnewater (p70)

★ Top Experiences

The Journey Begins Here

The Bs have it: romantic, canal-laced Bruges and buzzing, multinational Brussels are Belgium's unmissable duo. While Brussels dwarfs Bruges in size and cosmopolitan flair, both boast serene waterways, leafy parks, bustling markets, cutting-edge fashion, cycling trails, and galleries filled with homegrown art – from Flemish Primitives to Hergé's Tintin. Add the world's best beer and chocolate, plus that famous self-deprecating Belgian sense of humour, and you've got plenty of reasons to linger.

Mélissa Monaco
@mellovestravels

Mélissa is a travel blogger and guide-book writer based in Brussels.

Helena Smith
@helenasmithpix

Helena loves to write about eco travel, community and the outdoors.

Markt (p38)

Architectural Experiences

From the medieval charms of Bruges to the urban chaos of Brussels, these two cities are chock-full of architectural wonders.

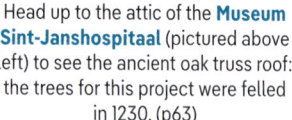

Head up to the attic of the **Museum Sint-Janshospitaal** (pictured above left) to see the ancient oak truss roof: the trees for this project were felled in 1230. (p63)

Look around one of Europe's most beautiful squares: the **Grand-Place** (pictured above right) with its gilded merchant houses and Gothic city hall. (p84)

Climb the massive tower of **Bruges' belfry**, still dominating the city and surrounding area after hundreds of years. (p38)

Be dazzled by the **house and workshop** of Victor Horta and its Art Nouveau details, from vine-like wrought iron to a luminous stained-glass skylight. (p135)

Right: Musée Horta (p135)

THE BEST

Museum Experiences

From Flemish Primitives to the making of fries, Belgium has hundreds of museums for all ages and interests.

Marvel at the sublime works by the masters of refined oil painting bedecking the **Groeningemuseum** (pictured above left). (p60)

See the applied arts collection at **Gruuthusemuseum**, a fairy-tale palace to rival Disney's best. (p66)

Get a sense of history, Europe's future and what unites Europeans at the **House of European History**. (p133)

Admire Breughel and Rubens at the Old Masters Museum, and Magritte's surrealism at Musée Magritte, two branches of **Musée Royaux des Beaux-Arts** (pictured above right). (p110)

Discover the Egyptian mummies, medieval tombs and Art Deco armchairs of **Musée Art & Histoire**, a treasure trove of world cultures. (p130)

Right: Totem pole created by Calvin Hunt and Mervyn Child, Canada, Kwakwaka'wakw community, Musée Art & Histoire (p130)

FROM LEFT: GROENINGE MUSEUM © MUSEUMS OF BRUGES, SALVADOR MANIQUIZ/SHUTTERSTOCK, IVAN YOHAN/SHUTTERSTOCK

THE BEST

Beer Experiences

Belgium is the land where the craft of brewing has become the stuff of legends. Taste them, in moderation, here.

Pull up a chair at the city's oldest bar, **Café Vlissinghe** (pictured above left), with an interior straight out of an Old Master painting. (p52)

Brace your taste buds for 11% Garre beer at the **De Garre** pub, hidden up a teeny alley. (p52)

Discover **Moeder Lambic** and its carefully curated list of beers, from *gueuze* to craft. (p104)

Enter the cellar bar **'t Poatersgat** (pictured above right) featuring umpteen Trappist beers to sample under the medieval arches. (p52)

Grab a fresh one at **Mazette**, a microbrewery-bakery in the heart of the Marolles. Beer is brewed downstairs, bread baked on site. (p124)

THE BEST

Dining Experiences

Sure, mussels and *frites* (fries) are delicious but have you tried Brussels and Bruges' best culinary treats? No wonder they are regarded as serious foodie destinations.

Indulge at **LESS Eatery** and its shared food concept of bold, globetrotting flavours by Michelin-starred chef Gert De Mangeleer. (p75)

Enjoy Elliott Van de Velde's cuisine at **Entropy**, where a six-course plant-based menu meets surprising organic wines. (p103)

Taste the freshest of fish served up at **De Stove**, where every element on the menu is lovingly handmade. (p51)

Have lunch or dinner in a cosy Marolles house at **La Bonne Chère**, serving seasonal menus and Moldovan wines inspired by the chef's roots. (p122)

LESS Eatery (p75)

COURTESY OF LESS EATERY

THE BEST

Picture-Perfect Experiences

Everybody loves a good photo. Whether it's an intimate corner of town or a sweeping view, get ready for some pretty decent photo ops.

Step into Bruges' **Volkskundemuseum** (pictured above left), a charming folk museum inside a marvellous old *godshuis* (almshouse), one of the neighbourhood's many quaint buildings. (p49)

Gaze from the **Gruuthusemuseum**'s balcony for sublime arcaded views of the Saint-Bonifaciusbrug bridge. (p66)

Visit the **Galeries Saint-Hubert** early, as the morning light floods through the glass roof. (p94)

Travel back in time in the almost-hidden **Rue de la Cigogne**, a miraculously preserved and atmospheric little street. (p93)

For a panoramic picture opportunity of Brussels, go to the top of the **Mont des Arts** (view pictured above right) just before sunset. (p118)

Right: Gruuthusemuseum (p66)

THE BEST

Outdoor Experiences

Although both cities are tightly built-up, Bruges breathes with its canals and Brussels with its many green spaces, allowing visitors to enjoy the outdoors.

See the city by water on a 30-minute **boat tour**. Boats depart roughly every 20 minutes from jetties south of Markt and Burg. (p72)

Stroll or bike around the romantic **Minnewater**, aka the 'Lake of Love', and bring a picnic basket. (p70)

Fancy a run? You won't be alone jogging the shaded alleyways of the **Parc de Bruxelles**. (p118)

Walk through the lively **Marolles** district, where the Breughel street-art trail leads you past colourful murals, fitting tributes to this famous painter. (p116)

Minnewater (p70)

YURY DMITRIENKO/SHUTTERSTOCK

THE BEST

Shopping Experiences

Whether it's food, drinks, vintage stores, antiques or quirky souvenirs, Brussels and Bruges are a shopper's paradise.

Salivate at **Diksmuids Boterhuis** (pictured above left), a gorgeous traditional grocery selling cheeses, honey, cold meats and mustard. (p54)

Sip your way through **Bacchus Cornelius**, a quirky shop where local beers and *jenevers* share space with antiques and pianos. (p54)

Try Belgian delicacies at **D'EN Belge**, especially beers and wines. When the weather's nice, the friendly owner opens his terrace. (p105)

Browse souvenirs **Manneke** (pictured above right). Everything is locally made, creative and far from the usual tourist trinkets. (p105)

Be on the lookout for prehistoric fossils to quirky 1970s lava lamps at **Passage 125**, one of Brussels' largest antique stores. (p125)

SOBERKA RICHARD/ALAMY

Concertgebouw (p72)

THE BEST
Wet-Weather Experiences

Sure, Belgium's weather is not its strong suit, but rainy days are no reason to mope. Brussels and Bruges are packed with things to do indoors.

Catch a foreign film at Bruges' arthouse **Cinema Lumière**, then visit the loo with its unique medieval tower view. (p49)

Take a tour of the **Concertgebouw**, one of the few contemporary buildings in Bruges, and its art collection. (p72)

Lose yourself in books at **Passa Porta**, a large, multilingual bookshop, and maybe catch a literary event there. (p93)

Enjoy a blockbuster film, and the golden glory of the 1930s Grand Eldorado theatre, at the **UGC De Brouckère** cinema. (p98)

Best for Kids

Kick-start your kids' interest in history and bring the tangled tale of Bruges to life with **Historium** museum's exciting VR exhibits. (p38)

Eat your way through the delicious and surprisingly interesting **Choco-Story** museum, then wait for the crash after the sugar high. (p50)

Take a summer plunge with the kids from a wooden pontoon into the waters of the **Coupure Canal**. (p72)

Keep the little ones (and little ones at heart) entertained at the **Institut des Sciences Naturelles** and its dinosaurs. (p136)

Become a chocolatier for a day thanks to the **Belgian Chocolate Makers** workshop. (p97)

Learn all about Belgian comics and their heroes (Tintin, the Smurfs) and marvel at this Horta building at the **Centre Belge de la Bande Dessinée**. (p90)

Best for Free

Wander the path circling the tree-filled courtyard of the **Begijnhof** in Bruges and breathe in the serene atmosphere. (p70)

Get to know Bruges on one of the highly recommended **Legends Walking Tours**. (p48)

Visiting the magnificent **Onze-Lieve-Vrouwekerk** is free of charge, but getting close to Michelangelo's *Madonna* is not. (p70)

Take the elevator to the **58 Rooftop&Eatery** for the best view over Brussels. No need to buy a drink if you're just checking the panorama. (p104)

Book a visit to the **Parlamentarium** and get to know how the EU Parliament works. (p132)

Tour the **European Parliament** and witness European democracy in action. (p132)

Perfect Days

Brussels and Bruges brim with architecture, museums, parks and an appreciation for life's finer things. Deciding where to start can be tricky, so we've made it easier for you.

Cathédrale Saints-Michel-et-Gudule (p87)

DAY ONE

Only Have One Day in Brussels?

MORNING

Begin your tour at the magnificent **Grand-Place** (p84). Visit the ornate **Hôtel de Ville** (p84) and explore the **Galeries Saint-Hubert** (p94) before reaching the **Cathédrale Saints-Michel-et-Gudule** (p87).

AFTERNOON

Enjoy a meal with a view over Brussels at **albert** (pictured above; p122), then explore the Old Masters at **Musée Royaux des Beaux-Arts** (p110). Unwind with a late-afternoon stroll in **Parc de Bruxelles** (p118).

EVENING

Time your evening with the sunset: sip an aperitif with panoramic views at **58 Rooftop&Eatery** (p104), then enjoy a classic Belgian dinner at **Bouillon Bruxelles** (p102).

DAY TWO

DAY THREE

A Weekend Trip to Brussels

MORNING

On your second day, get up early for the Marolles' daily **flea market** (p117) and antique shops, admire **Cité Hellemans** (p117), and refuel with coffee or brunch at alternative **Chaff** (p124) or vegan hotspot **Lucifer Lives** (p122).

AFTERNOON

Explore the rich antiquity collections at the **Musée Art & Histoire** (p130), admire dinosaurs at the **Institut des Sciences Naturelles** (p136) or learn about the EU at the **Parlamentarium** (p132).

EVENING

Start your evening at **Le Cirio** (p103), followed by a traditional puppet show at **Théâtre de Toone** (pictured above; p100). Have dinner at funky **Kline** (p102) and conclude your night with a cocktail at legendary **L'Archiduc** (p104).

One Day in Bruges

MORNING

Wander through the Sint-Anna district, visiting Jeruzalemkerk and the **Volkskundemuseum** (p49). Stroll over to **Blackbird** (p51) on Jan Van Eyckplein for a healthy lunch and to people watch.

AFTERNOON

Press on to the **Museum Sint-Janshospitaal** (p63) and its world-renowned Memling paintings. Wander through **Minnewater** (pictured above; p70) park to **De Stoepa** (p74) for an aperitif in its agreeable courtyard.

EVENING

Dine at vibrant **L'Estaminet** (p75; book ahead). Catch a show at **Concertgebouw** (p72), then end your evening with a romantic walk under gas-lit lamps to **De Republiek** (p53) for a nightcap.

If You Have More Time in Bruges

Stroll past the **Vismarkt** (p54) along the famous canals. Ascend the **Belfort** (p38) for panoramic views and visit the **Basiliek van het Heilig Bloed** (p43) to see Bruges' holiest relic, then the **Onze-Lieve-Vrouwekerk** (p70) church for a view of Michelangelo's *Madonna with Child*.

———————————————

Enjoy a local lunch at **De Belegde Boterham**, then appreciate Belgian art at the **Groeningemuseum** (p60). Take a leisurely stroll in the tranquil **Begijnhof** (p70) and explore its charming house museum. Tour **Brouwerij De Halve Maan** (p71), the brewery behind Brugse Zot.

If you've not indulged too much, have a drink at the city's oldest pub, the picturesque **Café Vlissinghe** (p52). Feeling hungry and flush? Have dinner at glamorous **LESS Eatery** (p75), with its minimalistic-chic Japan-inspired decor, or local fare at **Gran Kaffee De Passage** (p51). Wrap up the night at **Joey's** (p53) for some live music.

Basiliek van het Heilig Bloed (p43)

IVAN SOTO COBOS/SHUTTERSTOCK

A City Day Trip

Carry an umbrella like the locals! In Brussels, visit the **Brussels City Museum** (p86) in the Maison du Roi to uncover the city's history. See the original Manneken Pis (pictured above left; the one outside is a replica) and pop into his quirky **GardeRobe** (p89).

In Bruges, brighten a grey day at the **Frietmuseum** (p50), dedicated to the story of the humble potato and Belgium's beloved chips, with a free tasting at the end. Sweet tooth? **Choco-Story** (p50) showcases why Belgian chocolate is world-famous, complete with samples to prove it.

On a Rainy Day

Hop on the train to **Ostend** (pictured above right) to visit the house museum dedicated to symbolist artist **James Ensor** and do the museum's app-guided walk, or take the **Marvin Gaye Midnight Love Tour**. Have a relaxed lunch at **Bistro Beau-Site**, overlooking the North Sea.

Take the coastal tram a few stops west to **Atlantikwall Raversyde** to explore fascinating wartime bunkers. Back in Ostend, scoot along the promenade on a go-kart or family quadricycle. Have chips from **Frituur Franky** on the seafront, and round things off with a Trappist beer at **Lafayette Music Bar**.

Get Prepared

BOOK AHEAD

Three months before
Book ahead if you plan to attend a concert, or the opera at La Monnaie.

One month before
Make your dinner reservations – especially if visiting over a weekend – and book your beer spa experience.

One week before
Book a guided tour or an early-bird nightclub ticket.

Manners Matter

Belgians are quite relaxed and easy-going but dislike pretentiousness and tardiness (except for a house party where it's OK to be 'fashionably late'). Feeling spontaneous? It's best not to drop by on someone unannounced. Call ahead of time, as Belgians value planning.

Finally, don't assume that everybody can speak French in Flanders. When in doubt, it's fine to use English.

Managing the Bill

When you feel ready to leave a restaurant, ask for the bill – it won't come automatically. In Belgium, dining is a way to relax and socialise, so take your time. When asked about coffee or a *digestif*, take the opportunity to request the bill. Splitting is usually fine, but some places may not accept a mix of cash and card – ask ahead to avoid any surprises.

Things to Know

Bring an umbrella or waterproof jacket. With an average of 200 rainy days per year in Belgium, you never know what to expect so it's best to be like the Belgians: prepared.

The Gare du Midi and Gare du Nord train stations in Brussels can be a bit rough at night. Stay alert and take public transport or a taxi to reach your destination.

Wear comfortable shoes, as the cobbled streets in Bruges and Brussels aren't the best places for high heels – save them for a special occasion.

Want to fit in? When ordering *frites* (fries) at a *frituur* (chip shop), ask for a side of Andalouse sauce (a mayonnaise-based sauce with tomato, onions and bell peppers).

TIPPING

Bills include tax and service. Tipping isn't required unless service is exceptional.

Restaurants	**Bars, pubs and cafes**	**Taxis**	**Hotel staff**
For excellent service	Round to the nearest euro	Round to the nearest euro	

DAILY BUDGET

Budget: less than €150

- Bed in a hostel dorm: €40
- *Frites* and a side or cheap meal: €12–21
- Museum admission: €10–15
- Public transport cap per day: €8

Midrange: €150–300

- Double room in a hotel: €80–200
- Two-course dinner and glass of wine: €60–80
- Guided tour: from €15
- Nightclub entry: €10–20

Top End: more than €300

- High-end apartment or hotel room: from €200
- Three-course dinner at a top restaurant: from €100
- One-hour beer spa: from €99
- Concert or opera ticket: €79–149

Currency
Euro (€)

Languages
Dutch in Bruges and French in Brussels (Brussels is officially bilingual but French is the most widely spoken language)

Time
CET — Central European Time (UTC +1 hour) late October to late March. CEST — Central European Summer Time (UTC +2 hours) late March to late October.

TIP

In Brussels, many museums offer free admission either on the first Wednesday afternoon or the first Sunday of the month. Be sure to check beforehand. Remember that most museums are closed on Monday.

📅 When to Go

Belgium's temperate climate makes it enjoyable year-round, though November to February can be gloomy. Bruges and Brussels are delightful in December with their Christmas markets.

Belgium is known for its rainy, unpredictable weather, so remember to pack an umbrella or a raincoat, no matter the season.

Both cities swarm with tourists between May and September and during the weekend. Try to avoid these periods or visit during the week if you can.

Late September and October are ideal times to go as there will still be sunny days (and that warm autumn glow that photographers like) but fewer crowds. In Bruges, consider the end of March/early April to witness the Begijnhof's daffodils in full bloom.

Festivals in Brussels

May It's hard to choose between the blue notes filling every corner of the capital during **Jazz Weekend** or the extravagant **Brussels Pride** where tens of thousands of LGBTIQA+ people and their allies party after a week of conferences.

July The **Ommegang** (p96), reen-acts the visit of Emperor Charles V and his son and heir, Philip, in 1549. It features a costumed procession and performances, and ends up with a great finale on the Grand-Place.

September Of course, Brussels had to organise an event celebrating the country's pride and joy: beer. Over 50 breweries across the Grand-Place invite you to sample their products during **Belgian Beer Weekend**.

December When the nights get long, **Winter Wonders** (p100) warms up the hearts with over a month of Christmas markets,

Brussels Weather

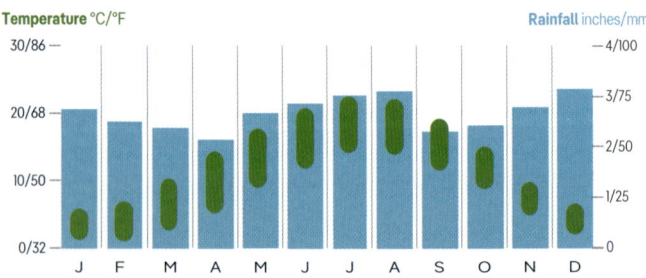

Winter Wonders (p100)

ice-skating, festive lights, a sound-and-light show and good cheer all around.

Festivals in Bruges

April 2027 Triënnale Brugge (p73) is a contemporary art event held every three years, where artists and architects use Bruges as their playground.

May The large Catholic **procession of the Holy Blood** (p43) dates back to the Middle Ages. At the heart of the procession is a cloth reputedly stained with the blood of Jesus Christ, brought to Flanders in the 12th century. It takes place each Ascension Day.

July An unexpectedly funky (for Bruges) event, the **Cactus Music Festival** (p73) sees big names and indie bands playing in Minnewater Park.

August Early music festival **Musica Antiqua** (p73) includes not only concerts but also hands-on workshops, such as harpsichord maintenance.

ACCOMMODATION LOWDOWN

There are no real low or high seasons, although prices can vary, especially in Bruges where summer is peak time for tourism. Brussels is a 'congress town'; rates may be a bit cheaper on weekends, but prices can jump during large events.

✈ Getting There

Most international travellers arrive in Belgium via Brussels Airport or Brussels South Charleroi Airport. Many also come by train and bus. Cruise ships occasionally dock at Brussels and Zeebrugge.

From the Airport to the City Centre

Train: Brussels Airport to Brussels or Bruges

This is easiest and fastest. Trains leave from level 1 at Brussels Airport.

Brussels Several trains per hour take you to the city centre in about 18 minutes, stopping at Nord, Central and Midi stations (€11.20 one way).

Bruges There's a direct train every hour (one hour 24 minutes), or change at a Brussels station (€26.10 one way).

Taxi: Brussels Airport to Brussels

The airport is only 13km from the centre. Taxis are easy to find at the official pick-up zone on the arrivals level. For rideshares, just follow the app's instructions.

Bus: Brussels Airport to Brussels

Bus 12 (STIB/MIVB) leaves from level 0 and takes you to Schuman Metro station (European Quarter). You can carry on to the city centre with the same ticket (€7.90 from the airport, €2.30 from the city centre).

Shuttle: Charleroi Airport to Brussels or Bruges

Coming in through Brussels South Charleroi Airport? The Flibco shuttle takes you straight to Brussels Midi or Bruges Sint-Pieters stations. Look for the signs at arrivals; to Brussels it's €18.90. To Bruges, fares start from €22.40. Book ahead.

Other Points of Entry

Arriving by Train or Bus

Most international trains to Brussels, like the Eurostar, arrive at Gare du Midi. From there, take public transport to the centre or catch a train to Bruges' Sint-Pieters. From Bruges' Sint-Pieters station, walk 20 minutes to the centre or hop on a De Lijn bus or taxi. Depending on your route, international buses may stop at Bruxelles-Nord, Bruxelles-Midi or Bruges Sint-Pieters.

Cruise Terminals

Brussels Cruise Terminal is a five-minute walk from the Chemin Vert tram stop (line 10 to the centre). From Zeebrugge, Cruise Express offers return shuttles to Bruges (€30 round trip; see cruise-express.be).

Getting Around

Brussels has a well-developed public transport network of metros, trams, buses and intra-urban trains. For late-night goers, Noctis buses and Collecto shared taxis are available.

Bruges is easily walkable but if you need them, buses by De Lijn (the Flemish public transport company) provide a reliable service, and taxis are also a good option.

Brussels

Metro, Tram & Buses All three systems are integrated under STIB/ MIVB, Brussels' public transport company. The metro is the fastest option, with two main lines (1 and 5) crossing east–west, plus circular line 2 and line 6 reaching the Heysel area. The partially underground tram lines 10 and 4 run through the centre from north to south. An extensive network of buses and trams provides additional coverage. Noctis night buses run on Friday and Saturday nights. Tickets work across all modes (transfers included) and are valid for one hour.

Train Brussels' 30 intra-urban stations are operated by the national railways company SNCB/NMBS.

These stations can be a time-saving option for reaching areas located far from the city centre. Children under 11 years accompanied by an adult ride free. If you plan to combine a train ride with STIB/MIVB metro, tram or bus services, be sure to purchase a Brupass ticket (€2.70) instead of the regular ticket (€2.30). The one-day pass also includes train travel within Brussels.

FROM LEFT: JJFARQ/SHUTTERSTOCK, HAND-ROBOT/GETTY IMAGES

— **ESSENTIAL APP** —

Brussels' STIB/MIVB: plan and buy tickets.
Floya: plan public transport all over Belgium and buy tickets for trains and De Lijn.

Shared Bikes & e-Steps Villo, Bolt and Dott are the three shared-bike services available. Bolt and Dott also operate e-scooters.

Taxis, Rideshares & Shared Taxis For long-distance, late-night transportation or if you have heavy luggage, taxis and rideshares are readily available. Be aware that not all taxis accept bank or credit cards. Collecto is a shared-taxi service picking up passengers at designated STIB/MIVB stops at a specific time during the night, and a great way to save if you're on a budget.

Bruges

Bus De Lijn buses provide decent service within Bruges. As the city is best explored on foot, you may wish to take a bus from Bruges Sint-Pieters station to the 't Zand bus station or line 1, which stops near the Markt.

Biking Blend in with the locals and rent a bike for a few hours or the day. It's the fastest way to discover the city.

Walking The real way to explore Bruges, just make sure you wear comfortable shoes.

Public Transport Essentials

In Brussels
Brussels' public transport system is run by STIB/MIVB, covering the metro, trams and buses. One ticket gives you access to all three for one hour, with unlimited transfers during that time.

There are three main ticket types:

STIB/MIVB Ticket – for travel only on the Brussels network (metro, tram, bus).

Brupass – ideal if you're also using the train or a De Lijn or TEC bus (the Flemish and Wallonian bus services) within the Brussels Capital Region.

Brupass XL – extends your travel to neighbouring areas just outside Brussels.

For single STIB/MIVB journeys, simply tap a contactless bank card or smartphone/smartwatch (Apple or Google Pay) on the grey validator inside stations or vehicles.

Prefer paper or need a Brupass? Pick up tickets at station machines or selected tram/bus stops. You can also buy Brupass tickets in the STIB/MIVB app – just don't forget to activate them before boarding.

Contactless fares are capped at €8.40 per day (equivalent to a one-day pass or four trips). Be sure to tap again when making connections.

If you're travelling only by train within Brussels, buy tickets through the SNCB or Floya app or at station machines.

In Bruges

In Bruges, buses are run by De Lijn. Hop on and tap your bank card or device on the onboard validator.

Digital tickets and passes are also available via the De Lijn or Floya app – just activate before boarding and show the screen to the driver.

Paper tickets can be bought at the De Lijnwinkel at Sint-Pieters station or at machines on 't Zand. All tickets are valid for one hour.

TRAVEL COSTS

Brussels Single Fare
€2.30 (contactless)
€2.80 (paper)

Brussels Train Ticket
€2.50

Bruges De Lijn Ticket
€3

─────── **IN BRUSSELS, TAP FOR TRANSFER** ───────

When transferring, don't forget to tap your contactless device or record it on the app.

TICKETS: BRUSSELS

Ticket Type	STIB/MIVB	Brupass	Train
Single fare	€2.30/2.80 (paper)	€2.70/3.70 XL	€2.50 (2nd class)/ 3.30 (1st class)
Day pass	€8.90	€9.50	
Airport2City	€7.90/8.40 (paper)		

TICKETS: BRUGES

Ticket Type	De Lijn
Single fare	€3
One-day pass	€9

🎁 A Few Surprises

Whoever said Belgium was boring, clearly does not know the country very well. Brussels and Bruges are full of quirks!

Art Nouveau–Inspired Transport

When Brussels' public transport company STIB/MIVB went through a full makeover, it embraced a unifying theme: Art Nouveau. The buses, trams and metro gleam in iron grey, bronze, gold and copper, echoing the metals beloved by the style. Even the hanging straps bear the elegant curves characteristic of the style. The result? A network so stylish it's scooped up several international design awards.

The Comic Strip Trail

Comic strips are deeply rooted in Belgium's history and psyche. After visiting the **Centre Belge de la Bande Dessinée** (p90), why not discover Brussels by following the **Parcours BD** *(parcoursbd. brussels),* the comics murals trail? Tintin, the Smurfs, Lucky Luke and many more bring colours to the walls of Brussels. There are over 70 murals spread around the city centre and beyond.

Tom Frantzen Statues

Brussels-born sculptor Tom Frantzen has a wicked sense of humour, and his bronze statues have become true city icons. *Het Zinneke* (Rue des Chartreux) sees a mutt lifting its leg on a bollard; *Jeanneke Pis* is the cheeky female answer to Manneken Pis. In Molenbeek, *Vaartkapoen* freezes a perfect slapstick moment: a rebellious youth tripping up a cop. At place de la Vieille Halle aux Blés, Jacques Brel belts out a song, arms wide open in *L'Envol* (The Flight) and nearby, meet Madame Chapeau, a Brussels theatre legend. Finally, don't miss Pieter Brueghel painting on an invisible canvas with a monkey perched on his shoulder. Together, these statues capture Brussels'

OFFBEAT BRUSSELS & BRUGES

Beer and wellness can mix! Soak in a hot beer tub at Brussels' **Bath & Barley** (p100).

Manneken Pis would put Kim K to shame. Check out his wardrobe of 1000+ costumes at his **GardeRobe** (p89).

See Bruges' spookiest church, **Jeruzalemkerk** (p48), and its grisly altarpiece decorated with skulls.

Don't do a runner, like Rubens did, from **Café Vlissinghe** (p52), Bruges' oldest pub. It's been serving pints since 1515.

Museum Sint-Janshospitaal (p63)

spirit – irreverent, theatrical and always self-deprecating.

mannequins thrown in for good measure.

Museum of Light

Bruges has a few off-the-wall museums (there's one dedicated to the humble chip for example), but **Lumina Domestica** (p49) is the most endearingly quirky – and genuinely illuminating. It features 6500 domestic lighting artefacts, starting with the history of fire-making and going up to ornate 20th-century lanterns, via terracotta Roman lamps. There's even a detour to explain the properties of luminous plants and animals: glow worms, fireflies and lantern fish. This is a private collection, and is interestingly jumbled rather than super slick, with a few spooky

Contemporary Art at the Hospital

A fallen archangel lying prone on an altar under its crumpled feathery wings, a woman tenderly cradling a monstrous multi-teated pig, a neon artwork calling for compassion; this is not a Hieronymus Bosch fever dream, it's the new modern art collection at **Museum Sint-Janshospitaal** (p63). Bruges may seem to pander to tourists with waffles and trinkets, but it's not afraid to take bold steps with its major museums. The peerless collection of works by Hans Memling is now complemented by contemporary art, which draws visitors into a new conversation with an ancient building.

Explore Bruges

Bruges' Walking Tours

Canal boat tour, Bruges
SERGII FIGURNYI/SHUTTERSTOCK

See p51

for eating,
drinking and
shopping
listings

Explore
Markt, Burg & North Bruges

Researched by
Helena Smith

Encircled by a major canal that loops for almost 9km around the old town, the geographical and spiritual heart of Bruges centres upon the adjacent Markt and Burg areas, linked by Breidelstraat. Here you'll find the mainstay of the city's medieval sights: the signature Belfort tower, gabled Brugse Vrije with its golden statues, the fantastical gilded Stadhuis and venerable Basiliek van het Heilig Bloed – where a reliquary is said to contain drops of Christ's blood. Locals refer to the 'north' as the area including Markt, Burg and all points north within the loop, also known as the city vests (*vesten* in Dutch).

Getting Around

Bus

Coming from the station, hop on city bus #1 or #2, both of which run through the city centre (you can make contactless payments on board). Buses are frequent enough that you can usually get a seat and enjoy the view; the service is operated by **De Lijn** (*delijn.be/en*) and runs from 5.30am to 11pm.

 On foot

The medieval city centre of Bruges is compact and walkable.

Car

Entry to the medieval centre is banned or restricted from 1pm to 6pm; driving is best avoided in Bruges.

THE BEST

TOWER
Belfort (p38)

BAROQUE BUILDING
Brugse Vrije (p41)

FACADE
Stadhuis (p42)

UNUSUAL CHURCH
Jeruzalemkerk (p48)

CHOCOLATE EXPERIENCE
Choco-Story (p50)

Brugse Vrije (p41)
RA FOTOGRAFIA/SHUTTERSTOCK

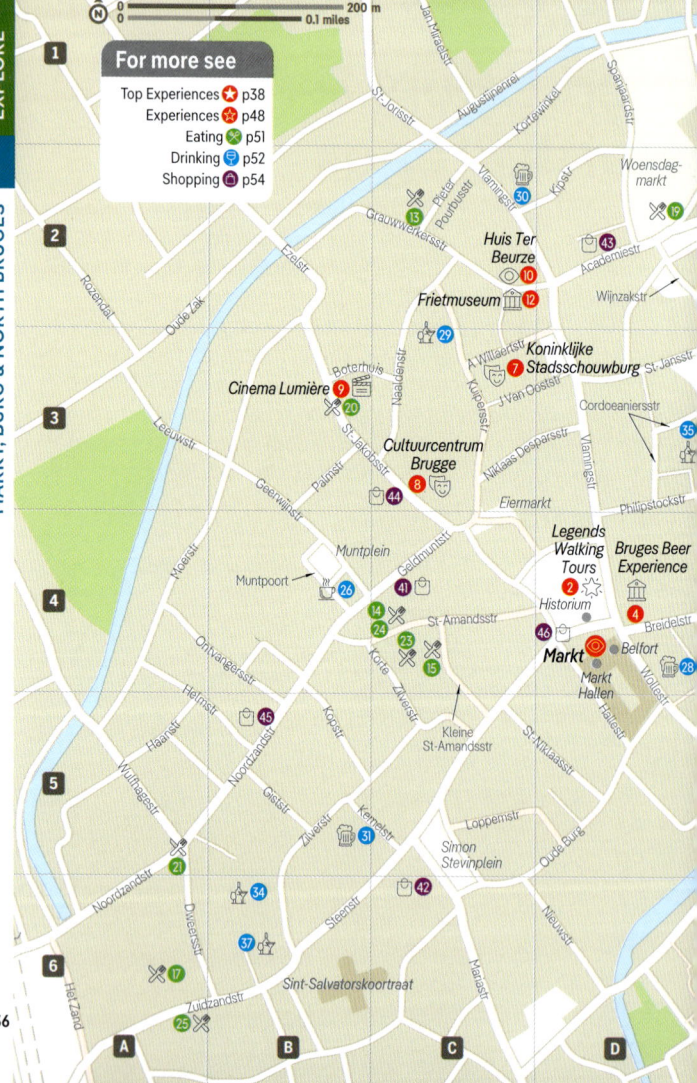

A   B   C   D

1

0 ——————— 200 m
0 ——————— 0.1 miles

For more see

Top Experiences ⭐ p38
Experiences 🏵 p48
Eating ✕ p51
Drinking 🍺 p52
Shopping 🛍 p54

Woensdag-markt

St-Jorisstr

Jan Miraelstr

Augustijnenrei

Kortewinkel

Kipstr

Spanjaardstr

Rozendal

Ezelstr

Oude Zak

Grauwwerkerstr

Peter Pourbusstr

Vlamingstr

13

30

Huis Ter Beurze 👁 10

43 Academiestr

Wijnzakstr

Frietmuseum 🏛 12

29

Boterhuis

A Willaertstr

Klipersstr

J Van Ooststr

Koninklijke Stadsschouwburg 7

St-Jansstr

Cordoeaniersstr

Cinema Lumière ✕ 9

Naaldenstr

St-Jakobsstr

20

Leeuwstr

Palmstr

Geerwijkstr

Cultuurcentrum Brugge 8 44

Niklaas Desparsstr

Vlamingstr

Eiermarkt

Philipstockstr

35

Muntplein

Muntpoort ☕ 26

Geldmuntstr

41 🛍

14

24

St-Amandsstr

23

15

Legends Walking Tours 2 ✨

Historium

Bruges Beer Experience 🏛 4

46

Markt ◎

Belfort

Breidelstr

28

Markt Hallen

Wollestr

Hallestr

Ontvangersstr

Helmstr

Haanstr

Wulfhagestr

45

Noordzandstr

Gistelstr

Korte

Zilverstr

Kleine St-Amandsstr

St-Niklaasstr

Loppemstr

Oude Burg

21

Zilverstr

Kemelstr

31

Simon Stevinplein

34

42

37

Sleenstr

17

Sint-Salvatorskoorstraat

Mariastr

Nieuwstr

25

Zuidzandstr

Dijverstr

Noordzandstr

Het Zand

A   B   C   D

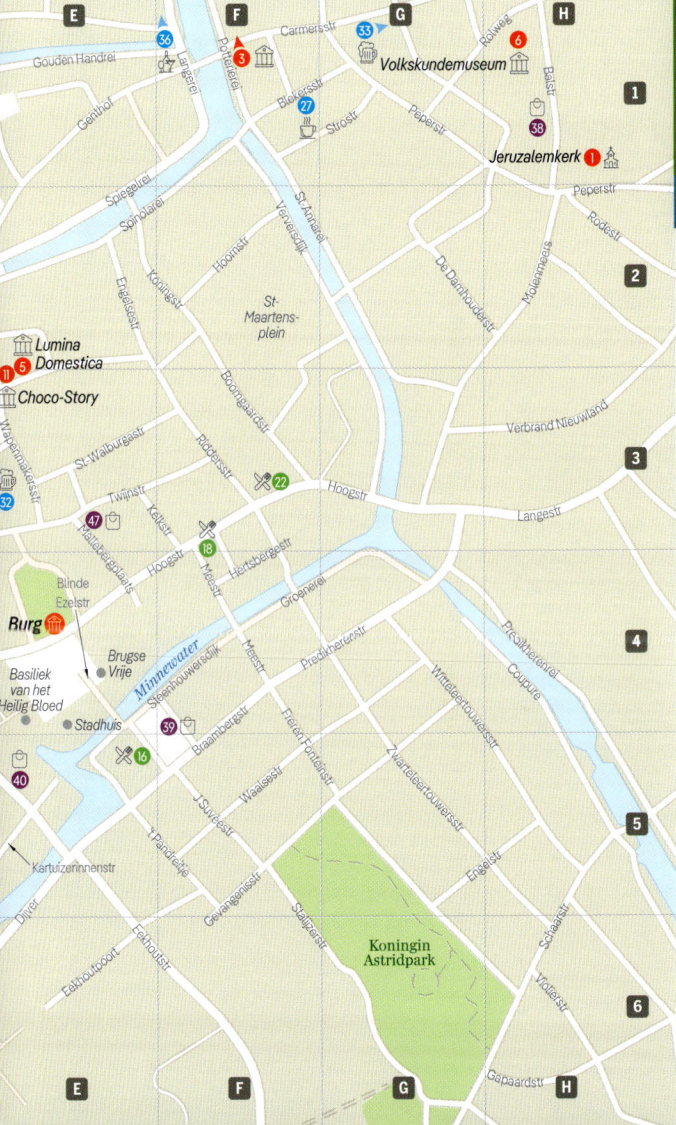

E   F   G   H

Carmersstr

Volkskundemuseum

Gouden Handrei

Rolweg

Balstr

Lazarij

Blekersstr

Stöstr

Peperstr

Jeruzalemkerk

Peperstr

Genthof

Spiegelrei

Spinolarei

Sint-Annarei

Koningstr

Hoornstr

St-Maartens-plein

Rodestr

De Damhoudtstr

Molenmeers

Engelstr

Waelmakersstr

Lumina Domestica

Choco-Story

Boomgaardstr

Verbrand Nieuwland

St-Walburgstr

Ridderstr

Hoogstr

Langestr

Twijnstr

Kelkstr

Mallebergplaats

Hoogstr

Hertsbergestr

Groenerei

Predikherenrei

Predikherenstr

Coupure

Blinde Ezelstr

Burg

Minnewater

Steenhouwersdijk

Wijnzakstr

Pieter-Pourbusstr

Witteleertouwersstr

Zwarteleertouwersstr

Basiliek van het Heilig Bloed

Brugse Vrije

Stadhuis

Braambergstr

Waalsestr

J.Suvéestr

Engelstr

Schaarstr

Kartuizerinnenstr

Eekhoutstr

't Pandreitje

Gevangenisstr

Slachtstr

Koningin Astridpark

Vrolestr

Gapaardstr

E   F   G   H

★ **TOP EXPERIENCE**

Markt

Flanked by medieval-style buildings, this splendid market square is the nerve centre of Bruges, lined with pavement cafes beneath step-gabled facades. Horse-drawn carriages clatter between open-air restaurants, watched over by Bruges' spectacular Belfort and the verdigris-green statue of the leaders of the Matins of Bruges revolt.

MAP P36 **D4**

PLANNING TIP
It's well worth purchasing a **Musea Brugge Card** *(concession/ adult €33/17),* which gives free entrance to the major museums in Bruges over a three-day period.

Scan this QR code to buy a Musea Brugge card.

Belfort

The symbol of Bruges is the UNESCO-listed, 13th-century Belfort (Belfry; *visitbruges.be/en; adult/ child €15/13),* rising a lofty 83m above the Markt. Ascending the belfry's 366 steps brings you past the treasury, the triumphal bell and a 47-bell, manually operated carillon, the chimes of which can be heard throughout the city. Once at the top, look out across the spires and red-tiled rooftops towards the wind turbines and giant cranes of Zeebrugge.

The belfry's 47-bell carillon is still played manually on a changing schedule (typically Wednesdays and weekends). Timings are posted on a signboard in front of the 13th-century **Markt Hallen**, the former market halls, where occasional exhibitions and fairs are hosted. You might also hear brass bands playing in the Markt.

Be sure to save some stamina for evening explorations. In summer, the building glows golden in the sun's late rays. And after dark is when Bruges is at its most magnificent, with lanes illuminated by gas lamps and dramatically floodlit architecture.

Historium

The Historium *(historium.be; adult/child €26/18)* occupies a fine neo-Gothic building on the northern

VISIT BRUGES © JAN D'HONDT

side of the square. Taking visitors back to 1435, it's an immersive multimedia experience, claiming to be more of a medieval movie than a museum. It's of most value for engaging those bored teens: a fictional love story provides engagement with the city's past. Visitors can also nose around a simulation of Jan Van Eyck's studio, among other pseudo-historic experiences.

Historium isn't heavy with facts, but it aims to provide a solid starting point for those just beginning to investigate the long and complex history of this medieval city. The most recent inclusion is a virtual-reality experience of time travel.

Market

Appropriately enough, this historical market square is still the location for a major farmers and flowers market, which is held on Wednesday

QUICK BREAK
Sample a huge array of Belgian beers at Rose Red (p53) on nearby Cordoeaniers-straat; the speciality is Trappist brews, and you can snack on tapas-style dishes.

MATINS OF BRUGES

The wealth and independence of Bruges' guildsmen created tensions with their French overlords. In 1302 the French sent a 2000-strong army to garrison Bruges. Undeterred, Pieter De Coninck and Jan Breydel led a revolt named the Matins of Bruges, creeping into town and murdering anyone who could not pronounce the Dutch phrase *'schild en vriend'* (shield and friend) in order to weed out French soldiers.

mornings. This is a venerable spot: the story of markets in the square dates back as far as the 13th century. Locals and tourists mingle to purchase cheeses, sausages, spit-roasted meat, fruit, vegetables and plants. The market runs from 8am to 2pm; come early and you get more of a local vibe. Authentic waffles are sold from a van, and the Belfort looms picturesquely over the proceedings. In winter, festive wooden chalets pop up selling mulled wine.

Eiermarkt

Immediately to the north, and adjoining Markt, this little **square** can be identified by a stone column surmounted by lions. The name means Egg Market: this is where eggs and dairy were sold in the past. The square is ringed by numerous bars and coffee shops, and compared to Markt, it's a marginally cheaper and less frenetic place for a coffee, or something stronger. Look out for the flamboyant 18th-century water pump, which once provided the people of Bruges with clean fresh water: a stone lion and bear hold Bruges' coat of arms, and weird snake-like creatures emerge from the mouth of a bearded and dishevelled bronze man.

Carriage Tours

Tours (*€70 for up to 5 people with payment in cash*) depart from Markt and take 30 minutes, with a pit stop at the Begijnhof (p70). While the carriages add some anachronistic charm to the square, there have been complaints about the expense of the trips, and the working conditions for the horses.

Burg

Just east of Markt, the less theatrical but still enchanting Burg has been the administrative centre of Bruges for centuries. In the square, which is dominated by the Stadhuis (Town Hall) and the Brugse Vrije, it's common to find public art installations that contrast the modern with the medieval. Burg's southern flank incorporates three superbly interlinked facades that glow with gilded detail. While their touristic pulling power is undeniable, these beautiful buildings are still very much part of the life of Bruges: the fairy-tale Stadhuis houses the city's administration offices, while Brugse Vrije stores the records of this ancient city.

MAP P36 **E4**

Brugse Vrije

The wonderful, eye-catching Brugse Vrije (*museabrugge.be/en; €3),* with its early baroque gables and golden statuettes, was once the seat of the 'Liberty of Bruges' – the large autonomous territory that was ruled from Bruges between 1121 and 1794. The territory was considered a major power in Flanders, alongside Bruges, Ghent and Ypres, up until its eventual abandonment. The building still houses city offices and stores city records, making it a treasure chest for Bruges' historians.

You can visit the Renaissancezaal to admire the remarkable carved chimney piece from 1531. Above a black-marble fireplace and alabaster frieze, the incredibly detailed oak carving depicts a sword-waving Emperor Charles V flanked by his grandfathers, Ferdinand of Aragon and Maximilian of Austria, both of whom sport extremely flattering codpieces.

To reach a photogenic spot by the canal, wander along pretty Blinde Ezelstraat between the Brugse Vrije and the Stadhuis.

PLANNING TIP
Burg is at its most tranquil and beautiful in the early evening and at night. See the sights, then hang around for a sunset stroll.

Scan this code to book a city walking tour.

VISIT BRUGES © JAN D'HONDT

QUICK BREAK
Try tiny De Garre (p52) for local brews with a local crew. It's tucked away down a narrow alley between Markt and Burg.

Stadhuis

The beautiful 1420 Stadhuis (pictured above; *visitbruges.be/en/stadhuis-city-hall; adult/child €8/4*) has a fanciful facade covered with replica statues of the counts and countesses of Flanders (the originals were torn down in 1792 by French soldiers). The facade is second only to Leuven's for exquisitely turreted Gothic excess.

Inside, an audio guide explains the figures in the many portraits before leading you upstairs to the astonishing Gotische Zaal, a dazzling hall with polychrome ceiling, hanging vaults, and romantic murals depicting historical scenes.

In an adjoining room, an augmented-reality display – based on research from the University of Ghent – dynamically illustrates the city's changing and sometimes perilous relationship with the sea. While the North Sea brought the city trade and immense wealth, silting and the tides at times threatened its very existence.

Basiliek van het Heilig Bloed

The western end of the Stadhuis morphs into the Basiliek van het Heilig Bloed (Basilica of the Holy Blood; *holyblood.com; treasury €5*), which takes its name from the few drops of Christ's blood supposedly contained within a phial that was brought here after the crusades in the 12th century. The right-hand door leads up to a colourful chapel, where the relic is hidden behind a flamboyant silver tabernacle.

Also upstairs is the basilica's one-room treasury, where you'll see the jewel-studded reliquary in which the phial is mounted on Ascension Day for Bruges' biggest annual parade, the **Heilig-Bloedprocessie**. This large Catholic procession of the 'Holy Blood' dates back to the Middle Ages, and takes place each Ascension Day (40 days after Easter). The relic is brought out for veneration at 2pm daily – respectful and quiet visitors are welcome.

Downstairs, entered via a different door, is the basilica's contrasting bare-stone 12th-century Romanesque chapel, a meditative place that's almost devoid of decoration.

Vismarkt

South of Burg and across the bridge, the lovely 1821 Vismarkt (p54) building still accommodates fish stalls on Tuesday to Saturday mornings, along with craft and trinket sellers later in the day. The attractive columned and colonnaded building with its stone slabs was created when complaints about the smell from the fish stalls on the Markt got too vociferous.

Several seafood restaurants here back onto pretty Huidenvettersplein, where archetypal Bruges buildings include the old tanners' guildhouse.

SHOP LIKE A LOCAL

Central Bruges can sometimes feel like a melee of waffle stands and *frites* (fries) stalls. But it's worth remembering that this is indeed a real place, where discerning locals do their shopping, eating and drinking. If you're on the hunt for interesting beers, cheeses and charcuterie, as well as vintage clothes and bric-a-brac, there are some real gems to be found. See p54.

WALKING TOUR

Bruges Back Streets

Much of the magic of Bruges involves losing yourself in its warren of little lanes, picturesque canals and postcard-perfect streetscapes; the Belfort is a good landmark if you ever get lost. This route takes you on a gentle circuit of back streets, past some of the lower key attractions of this enticing city. Oh, and some amazing chocolate.

START	END	LENGTH
Markt	Markt	2.5km; 2–3hr

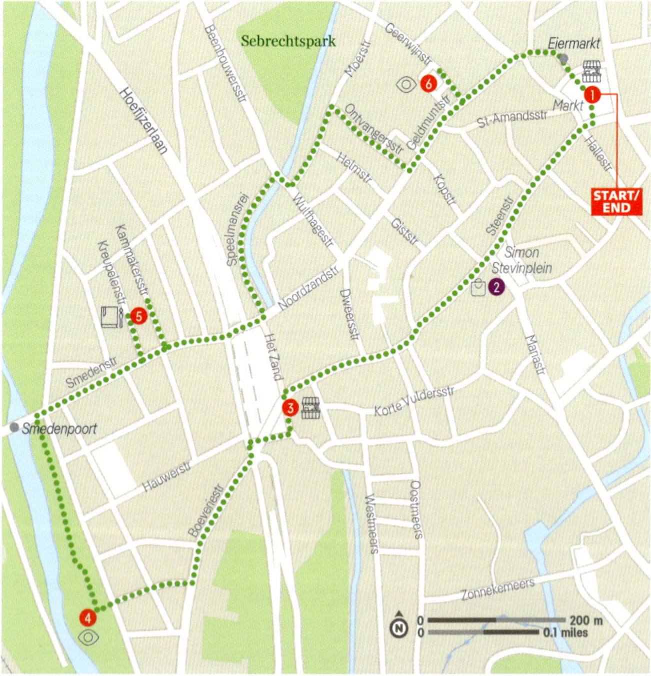

1 Markt Meander

Encompassing canals, almshouses and excellent chocolate, this walk starts at **Markt** (p38), Bruges' beating heart, with its fantastic neo-Gothic buildings and the soaring Belfort looming above. Take some time to dip into the sights here, and fuel up with a coffee at one of the many alfresco cafes.

Once you've wandered about the magnificent square, head for the street that leads southwest, Steenstraat, with its fine 17th-century facades.

2 Time for Chocolate

Detour into the attractive Simon Stevinplein square – named for 16th-century Bruges mathematician and physician Simon Stevin – on the right-hand side. Sample the wares at the **Chocolate Line** (p55); it's run by Dominique Persoone, who many regard as the city's most outrageous and innovative chocolatier. The surprising flavours include Cuban cigar and wasabi.

3 Saturday Market

Zuidzandstraat leads down to **Het Zand Square**. On Saturday mornings, it hosts a major market – which spills over onto nearby Beursplein (follow Hauwerstraat, heading west) – with food, flowers and everything from live chickens to rabbits being sold by regional vendors. If you're not here on market day, cross the refreshingly modern open square, bearing left onto Boeveriestraat.

4 Watery Bruges

Here the route approaches the water, where you'll see the scenic old **Waterhuis**. In the Middle Ages, horses operated a wheel here to pull water out of the canal, which was then used to supply wells and breweries. Turn right to take the path through the stretch of parkland, and soon you'll come to **Smedenpoort**, a 14th-century city gate.

5 Ancient Almshouses

Turn right, back in the direction of the city centre up Smedenstraat. A detour here up Kreupelenstraat or Kammakersstraat takes you to some typical Bruges **almshouses**.

Speelmansrei curves to the left, following the left bank of the canal for a stretch. Cross the canal and turn left onto Moerstraat, then right onto Ontvangersstraat. Head down and turn left onto bustling Noordzanstraat.

6 Gelato Detour

A final detour is to peek at little Muntplein off to the left, where locals gather to eat ice cream from Da Vinci. Then you join the attractive cafe-encircled mini-square of **Eiermarkt** (p40), which is the place to be for an early-evening beverage.

Time your return to Markt for nightfall, and you're in for a real treat – the dramatically floodlit buildings are a sight to behold.

WALKING TOUR

Sint-Anna Windmills

The district of Sint-Anna provides a delightful breather from central Bruges and an insight into the industrious past of the district. Here in the quiet alleys you'll begin to get a sense of Bruges' true beauty. There are stops at a folk museum, an intriguing church and windmills, and you'll find dainty handmade lace along the way.

START	END	LENGTH
Volkskundemuseum	OLV-ter-Potterie	2km; 2hr

1 Fun in the Folk Museum

The **Volkskundemuseum** (p49), set in a *godshuis* (almshouse), features 18 themed tableaux illustrating Flemish life in times gone by. It's a delightful place to wander, and you can play some old-school games and try on historic clothes. Stop at the quaint museum cafe De Zwarte Kat (p52) for cheap beer and snacks.

2 Lace Makers

Walking south along Balstraat, **Kantcentrum** *(kantcentrum.eu; adult/child €8/6)* displays a collection of lace; during the afternoon, you can watch bobbin lace being made by experienced lacemakers and their students. Once you've seen how intricate the process is, you'll swiftly understand why handmade lace is so expensive; a small piece costs €10.

A little further up the street, you can shop at 't Apostelientje (p54) if you'd like to take home some delicate authentic local lacework garments or gifts.

3 Jeruzalemkerk

Unless you scare easily, enter the Adornesdomein to the left of Kantcentrum and check out its fascinating family history museum and the macabre, dramatic **Jeruzalemkerk** (p48) on the corner. When you're done having a look here, turn left onto Peperstraat.

4 City Gate

Keep walking until you reach the fortified gate-tower **Kruispoort**, an impressive isolated remnant of the former city wall. Much restored and partially rebuilt, the city gate was originally constructed in the 13th century When you reach the gate, turn left and walk north.

5 Windmills

From the 13th century through to the 19th century, Bruges' ramparts were graced with *molens* (windmills); ambling along the canal bounding the eastern side of the city takes you through pretty parkland past two of Bruges' four remaining examples. First comes **Bonne Chieremolen** (not open to the public), followed by the 18th-century **Sint-Janshuismolen**, which still grind cereals into flour and houses a small museum. The sails are occasionally set in motion.

6 De Windmolen

From here, you'll be able to see the quaint corner bar-cafe **De Windmolen** (p53); it's the perfect spot to take a break and enjoy the outlook.

7 OLV-ter-Potterie

When you're done, follow Peterseliestraat northwest and then turn left and walk along the scenic Potterierei, where you'll find statues of the Madonna adorning every corner until you reach **Our Lady of the Pottery** (p48) church, your final stop.

EXPERIENCES

Get Spooked at Jeruzalemkerk
CHURCH

Within the so-called Adornesdomein estate is one of Bruges' oddest churches, the 15th-century **Jeruzalemkerk** (MAP: ① P36 H1; *adornes.org/en; adult/child €8/6*), built by the Adornes family. Supposedly based on Jerusalem's Church of the Holy Sepulchre, it's a macabre monument with a gruesome altarpiece covered in skull motifs and an effigy of Christ's corpse tucked away in the rear mini-chapel. The entry price includes admission to a small museum that occupies several pretty *godshuizen* (almshouses).

The estate, dating from 1429, remains in the ownership of the Adornes family. The Count and Countess Maximilien de Limburg Stirum are the 17th generation of descendants of Anselm Adornes, whose heart is enshrined in a black-marble tomb in the church – presumably the only remains that were able to be returned to Bruges after he was murdered in Scotland in 1483.

Walk with Legends
TOUR

Highly lauded operator **Legends Walking Tours** (MAP: ② P36 D4; *legendstours.be*) runs a series of wildly popular – and free – walking tours that are a great way to get oriented before making your own explorations of the city. Book online in advance for daily departures: a variety of time slots are offered. Tours depart in front of the statue in the Markt: look for the red umbrella.

Duck into OLV-ter-Potterie
CHURCH

Admission to **OLV-ter-Potterie** (MAP: ③ P36 F1; *visitbruges.be; adult/child €8/4*), a small historical church-hospital complex, is free with a Sint-Janshospitaal museum ticket. Ring the bell to gain entry and explore fine art from the 15th and 16th centuries. The lushly baroque church houses the reliquary of St Idesbaldus and a polychrome wooden relief of Mary breastfeeding baby Jesus. In later (more prudish) centuries, the Virgin's nipple

 LACE UP

If you're on the hunt for souvenirs, look out for the city's renowned, but rare, handmade lace. There are two methods of making lace (*kant/dentelle* in Dutch/French). Needlepoint lace (*naaldkant*) uses a single thread to build up an embroidered pattern over a 'ground' material. Originally Italian, the technique was perfected in Brussels, and the stitch is still known as 'corded Brussels'. In contrast, bobbin lace (*kloskant*) creates a web of interlinked threads using multiple threaded bobbins, twisted using hand-placed pins. It's an astonishingly fiddly process, believed to have originated in 14th-century Bruges, and it can still be seen at Bruges' Kantcentrum (p47).

received a lacy camouflage, rendering the scene bizarrely impractical.

Taste Bruges Brews
BEER

The Markt's newest attraction, **Bruges Beer Experience** (MAP: **4** P36 **D4**; *brugesbeermuseum.com; with/without 3 tastings €20/14*), will appeal to the many who love a Belgian beer. Guided by a multilingual iPad app, the museum takes you through the history of beer, the brewing process and the various different types of beers in Belgium and beyond. Three tastings are included, or you can opt out for a reduced admission. There is, of course, a gift shop.

Switch on at the Lamp Museum
MUSEUM

Lumina Domestica (MAP: **5** P36 **E2**; *luminadomestica.be; adult/child €18/11*), the enlightening Domestic Lamp Museum, has over 6500 artefacts relating to domestic lighting throughout history, making it the largest collection of its kind. It sheds light on the history of the humble lamp and illuminates awareness about the consumption and conservation of energy.

Folky Fun
FOLK MUSEUM

The appealing **Volkskunde-museum** (MAP: **6** P36 **H1**; Museum of Folk Life; *visitbruges.be; adult/child €8/4*) presents visitors with 18 themed tableaux illustrating Flemish life in times gone by and includes a 1930s sweetshop, a hatter's workshop, a traditional

ENTERTAINMENT

Koninklijke Stadsschouwburg
Opera, classical music, theatre and dance are on offer at this majestic **theatre** (MAP: **7** P36 **C3**) dating from 1869. Out front is a modern statue of Papageno from Mozart's *The Magic Flute*.

Cultuurcentrum Brugge
This **cultural group** (MAP: **8** P36 **C3**; *ccbrugge.be*) organises theatre productions, events and concerts, and coordinates performances at the Koninklijke Stadsschouwburg and Magdalenazaal. Check the website for what's on where and when.

Cinema Lumière
Just a couple of blocks back from the Markt, this **art-house cinema** (MAP: **9** P36 **B3**; *lumierecinema.be*) screens a well-chosen programme of foreign films in their original languages.

kitchen and more. The museum is a static affair, but it's in an attractive whitewashed *godshuis,* and the time-warp museum cafe De Zwarte Kat (p52) has a fine selection of beer. Temporary exhibits upstairs are often worth a look. Traditional lollies are made here on the first and third Thursday of the month.

Take Stock
NOTABLE BUILDING

It's believed that the world's first stock exchange began in and

Q-IMAGES/ALAMY

Dive into Chocolate's History

FOOD MUSEUM

The highly absorbing **Choco-Story** (MAP: ⑪ P36 **E3**; pictured left; *choco-story-brugge.be/en; adult/child €14/8.50*) chocolate museum traces the cocoa bean back to its role as an Aztec currency. Learn about choco history, watch a video on cocoa production and sample a praline that's made as you watch (last demonstration 4.45pm). Cheaper combination tickets with a variety of other museums are available.

Get Fried

FOOD MUSEUM

Follow the history of the potato from ancient Inca grave sites to Belgian fryers. The **Frietmuseum** (MAP: ⑫ P36 **C2**; *frietmuseum.be; adult/child €11/6.50*) entry fee includes a discount token for the basement *frituur* (chip shop) that immodestly claims to fry the world's ultimate chips. More interesting is the arch-gabled 1399 building itself, first used by Genoese traders, then by local weavers.

around the **Huis Ter Beurze** (MAP: ⑩ P36 **C2**), an elongated 13th-century house. It's not open to the public, but the space is used for special events and functions.

 BELGIAN CHOCOLATE

Fundamentally, chocolate is nothing but a mix of cocoa paste, sugar and cocoa butter in varying proportions. Dark chocolate uses the most cocoa paste; milk chocolate uses milk powder; and white chocolate uses cocoa butter but no cocoa paste. Mouthwatering Belgian chocolate is arguably the world's best because it sticks religiously to these pure ingredients, while other countries replace some of the cocoa butter with vegetable fats. The essential Belgian chocolates are pralines and creamy *manons* – filled, bite-sized chocolates sold from specialist shops. Assistants package up whatever chocolate you select from the display – it's fine to buy just one. Price varies radically according to the brand.

Best Places for...

Ⓔ Budget **ⒺⒺ** Midrange **ⒺⒺⒺ** Top End

See p36 for map of locations

Eating

Local Food

Pieter Pourbus ⒺⒺⒺ
⑬ C2

Located in an enchantingly whitewashed gabled building built in 1561, Pieter Pourbus is a wonderful spot for a cosy dinner, with beams, open fires and tiled floors. *pieterpourbus.com; 6-9pm Fri, Sat, Mon & Tue & noon-1.30pm & 6-9pm Sun*

Chagall ⒺⒺⒺ
⑭ C4

Seafood, including several variations on eel, is Chagall's forte, but it also does daily meat specials and good deals on two- and three-course menus. *restaurantchagall.be; noon-9pm Thu-Tue*

De Stove ⒺⒺⒺ
⑮ C4

Fish caught daily is the house speciality, but the monthly changing menu also includes the likes of wild boar fillet on oyster mushrooms. Everything, from bread to ice cream, is homemade. *restaurantdestove.eu; 7-9pm Fri, Sat, Mon & Tue, noon-1.30pm & 7-9pm Sun*

Den Gouden Karpel Ⓔ
⑯ E5

Take away or eat in, this sleek little pub/bar is a great location for a fresh seafood lunch, right by the fish market. *dengoudenkarpel.be; 11am-6pm Tue-Sat*

Gran Kaffee De Passage ⒺⒺ
⑰ A6

A menu of hearty traditional dishes, such as *stoverij* (local meat in beer sauce), at a candlelit, alternative, Art Deco–style bistro. *passagebruges.com; 5-11pm Tue-Thu & Sun, noon-11pm Fri & Sat*

Atelier D The Bistro ⒺⒺⒺ
⑱ F3

Tiny sophisticated bistro, with creative takes on French and Belgian staples. From the *graflax* starter to Wagyu and scallops then sabayon for dessert, the food looks and tastes exceptionally good. *atelierdthebistro.be; noon-1.30pm & 7-9pm Fri-Mon*

Vegan & Veggie Friendly

Blackbird Ⓔ
⑲ D2

A Bruges rarity: an all-vegan cafe serving bagels, bountiful happiness bowls, pancakes, fresh juices and cakes. *blackbird-bruges.com; 9am-3pm Wed-Sat, 9.30am-1pm Sun*

De Republiek ⒺⒺ
⑳ B3

This is a big, hipster modern bistro with great vegan choices. *republiekbrugge.be; noon-1am Wed-Sun, from 5pm Mon & Tue*

That's Toast ⒺⒺ
㉑ A5

Bruges' best breakfast restaurant has gained a following for its all-day brekkies, with several vegan options. *thatstoast.com; 8.30am-4pm Wed-Sun*

de Eenvoud
 22 F3

A soulful vegan deli where you can take away delicious soups, sandwiches and vegan cakes. There's also a tempting array of spreads and other goodies. *9.30am-5pm Tue-Fri*

Cafes & Bakeries

De Zwarte Kat ⊖
see **6** H1

This homely little cafe belonging to the Volkskundemuseum is a quaint spot for a light lunch, local beer or coffee and cake. *11.45am-2pm*

Gingerbread Tea Room ⊖
23 C4

A friendly pink-and-white cafe known for its bagel breakfasts, waffles, strong coffee and global range of teas. *9am-5pm*

Mey's Art Cafe ⊖
24 C4

Endearingly quirky place in the centre of town with a 1950s vibe and colourful paintings. Friendly staff dish up croque-monsieurs and waffles straight to your eye-poppingly colourful table. *meysart.be; 8.30am-6pm Thu-Tue*

Panos ⊖
 25 A6

This branch of Belgium's most popular bakery

chain has plenty of seating and is good when you need a snack in a hurry. *7am-6.30pm Mon-Sat, 11am-6.30pm Sun*

Merveilleux ⊖⊖
26 B4

An elegant marble-floored tearoom where drinks come with a dainty homemade biscuit and sometimes a glass of strawberry ice cream or chocolate mousse. Pretty cakes and tea too. *merveilleux.eu; 10am-6pm*

Drinking

Beer Pubs

Café Vlissinghe
27 F1

Luminaries have frequented Bruges' oldest pub for 500 years; allegedly Rubens painted an imitation coin on the table here then did a runner. *cafevlissinghe.be; 11am-10pm Wed-Sat, to 7pm Sun*

De Garre
28 D4

Try the fabulous Garre draught beer, which comes with a thick floral head in a glass like a brandy balloon. *degarre. be; noon-midnight*

Le Trappiste
29 C3

A specialist Belgian beer pub (26 beers on tap) in an 800-year-old vaulted medieval cellar. *letrappistebrugge.com; 5pm-midnight Mon-Sat*

't Poatersgat
30 C2

A cross-vaulted cellar glowing with flickering candles. The 'Monk's Hole' has 120 Belgian beers on the menu, including a selection of Trappists. *poatersgat.be; 3pm-late*

't Brugs Beertje
31 B5

Legendary throughout Bruges and beyond for its hundreds of brews, this cosy *bruin café* (brown cafe; traditional pub; pictured right) is filled with old posters, and locals who seem part of the furniture. *brugsbeertje.be; 4pm-midnight Mon, Thu & Sun, to 1am Fri & Sat*

Cambrinus
32 E3

Hundreds of varieties of beer are available at this 17th-century sculpture-adorned brasserie-pub, as well as traditional Belgian and Italian-inspired snacks and meals. *cambrinus.eu; 11am-11pm Sun-Thu, to late Fri & Sat*

ARTERRA/GETTY IMAGES

De Windmolen

 G1

Quaint corner bar-cafe with a sunny terrace overlooking one of the Sint-Anna windmills. *10am-10pm Mon-Thu, to 1am Fri-Sun*

Bars

Cafédraal

 B6

Attached to an upmarket seafood restaurant, this remarkable cocktail bar is enclosed by beech hedges and red-brick gabled buildings. *cafedraal.be; 6pm-1am Tue-Thu, to 3am Fri & Sat*

De Republiek

see B3

Set around a courtyard comprising characterful brick buildings, this big, buzzing space is super popular with Bruggelingen. DJs hit the decks on weekends, and there's a long cocktail list. *republiekbrugge.be; noon-1am Wed-Sun, from 5pm Mon & Tue*

Rose Red

 D3

Outstanding beers from 50 of the best breweries in Belgium, served by informative staff. There are beers on tap and 150 bottles, or you can taste four beers for €10. *rosered.be/en, 11am-11pm Tue-Sun*

Live Music Bars

Du Phare

 F1

Tucked into the remains of one of Bruges' original town gates, this off-the-beaten-track tavern is known for live blues and jazz sessions. Bus 4 stops out the front. *duphare.be; 11.30am-late*

Joey's

 B6

This dark, intimate bar is a gathering spot for

Bruges' musos. You can sometimes catch live music here, or just chill out with a creamy Stevie cocktail or Joey's Tripel. *11.30am-late Mon-Sat*

Shopping

Crafts

't Apostelientje
38 H1

The delicate garments and gifts on sale are made from beautiful handmade authentic lace. An unusual opportunity to buy the real Bruges deal lace-wise. *apostelientje. be; 1-5pm Tue-Sat*

Vismarkt
39 F4

The stone slabs of the colonnaded 1821 fish market (pictured right) still accommodate fish stalls most mornings, along with craft-sellers later in the day. *7am-5pm Tue-Fri*

Mille-Fleurs
40 E5

A cornucopia of Flemish tapestries machine-made near Wetteren. It also sells throws, tapestry cushions, runners and doilies,

plus bags and purses. *millefleurstapestries.com; 10am-6pm Mon-Sat*

Food & Beer

Diksmuids Boterhuis
41 C4

Decked out with red-and-white gingham flounces and featuring a ceiling hung with sausages, this 1933 grocery sells cheeses, honey, cold meats and mustard. *diksmuidsboterhuis. be; 10am-12.30pm & 2-6.30pm*

Chocolate Line
42 C6

Wildly experimental flavours by 'shock-o-latier' Dominique Persoone include bitter cola, Cuban cigar, wasabi and black olive with basil. *thechocolateline.be; 10am-6pm*

Bacchus Cornelius
43 D2

Independent store with an open fire and pianos, selling beers and *jenevers*. *bacchuscornelius.com; 1-6.30pm*

Clothes

Lee: Loo
44 C3

Ethical shopping with a funky edge: this store

sells 'animal-friendly' fashion, accessories, books, music, art and plant-based toiletries. *leeloo.be; 10am-6pm Mon & Wed-Sat*

L'Heroine
45 C3

Beautiful silk print dresses, asymmetrical tailoring and sumptuous scarves and drapes – staff can help you combine pieces for a strong, idiosyncratic look. *lheroine.be; 10.30am-6pm Mon-Sat*

Books & Music

De Reyghere Reisboekhandel
46 D4

This fabulous, well-stocked travel bookshop has been in the same family for generations. *dereyghere.be; 2-6pm Mon, 9.30am-noon & 2-6pm Tue-Sat*

Rombaux
47 E3

Here since 1920, this large, family-run music shop specialises in classical, jazz, Flemish, folk and world music. It also sells sheet music and acoustic guitars. *rombaux.be; 11am-6pm Tue-Sat*

See p74 for eating, drinking and shopping listings

Explore
South Bruges

Researched by
Helena Smith

The neighbourhoods south of Markt are where to head if you're trying to escape the crowds. Here, the tightly knit central warren of lanes and alleys widens out into broader streets, where moonlight strolls take on a more romantic, subdued vibe than similar nocturnal wanderings around the awe-inducing, dramatically floodlit core.

A visit to the world-class art gallery Groeningemuseum is a must, and a wander around Museum Sint-Janshospitaal, where six masterworks by Flemish Primitive painter Hans Memling are displayed, comes highly recommended. It's also in the south that you'll find Bruges' begijnhof and its calm courtyard, as well as some of the city's finest parks and gardens.

Getting Around

 Bus
Arriving at Bruges station, get on board bus #1 or #2; you can make a contactless payment to get to the city centre. Frequent services, operated by **De Lijn** *(delijn.be/en),* run from 5.30am throughout the day till 11pm.

 **On foot**
One of the pleasures of the city is walking the streets: the centre is small and easy to see on foot.

 Car
Driving in Bruges is best avoided, as entry to the medieval core is either banned or restricted from 1pm until 6pm.

⭐
THE BEST

FLEMISH ARTWORKS
Groeningemuseum (p60)

MEMLING MASTERPIECES
Museum Sint-Janshospitaal (p63)

FAIRY-TALE PALACE
Gruuthusemuseum (p66)

BREWERY
Brouwerij De Halve Maan (p71)

SWIM
Coupure Canal (72)

Canal tours on the Rozenhoedkaai (p72)

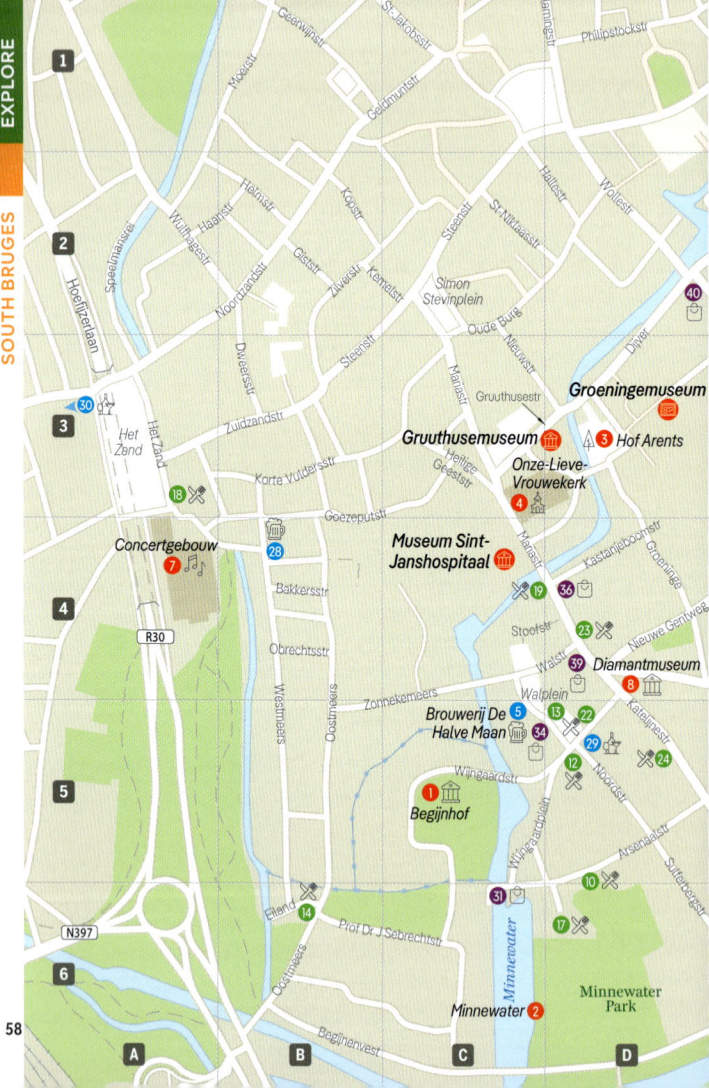

A 1
B 1
C 1
D 1

Geerwijnstr
St Jacobsstr
Geldmuntstr
Philipstockstr
Vlamingstr

A 2
B 2
C 2
D 2

Moerstr
Helmstr
Speelmansrei
Wulfhagestr
Haarstr
Noordzandstr
Giststr
Kuiperstr
Zilverstr
Kemelstr
Steenstr
St-Niklaasstr
Simon
Stevinplein
Oude Burg
Nieuwstr
Mariastr
Gruuthusestr

Diver

40

Groeningemuseum

A 3
30

Het Zand
Het Zand
Zuidzandstr

Duivelsstr

Gruuthusemuseum 🏛

Heilige
Geeststr

**Onze-Lieve-
Vrouwekerk**

4

🛆 3 *Hof Arents*

Korte Vulderstr

18 🍴

Goezeputstr

Steenstr

Mariastr

Kastanjeboomstr
Groeninge

Concertgebouw

7 🎵

🍺
28

Bakkersstr

**Museum Sint-
Janshospitaal** 🏛

19 🍴
36 🛍

R30

Obrechtstr

Stoofstr
23 🍴

39

Diamantmuseum
8

Walstr

Nieuwe Gentweg

Westmeers
Oostmeers
Zonnekemeers

**Brouwerij De
Halve Maan** 🏭

Walplein

13 🍴
5
34 🛍

22 🍴
29

12

24 🍴

Wijngaardstr

Noordstr
Katelijnestr

1

Begijnhof

Wijngaardplein

Eiland
14 🍴

Prof Dr J Sebrechtsstr

10 🍴

Arsenaalstr
Suikerkaai

31 🛍

17 🍴

N397

Begijnenvest

Minnewater 2

Minnewater

Minnewater
Park

A
B
C
D

58

E **F** **G** **H**

1

Hoogstr

Vulderstr

35

37

Coupure Canal 6

11

Ganzestr

Bilksle

2

9

Huiden-
vettersplein

26

Rozenhoedkaai

Braambergstr

Freren Fonteinstr

Wollestr

Wittelederhouwersstr

Coupure

Predikherenrei

Hoelstr

'tPandreitje

38

27

Zwartelederhouwersstr

Engelstr

Minderbroedersstr

Schaarstr

Vlzelstr

Koningin Astridpark

Stalijnstr

Violierstr

Gaparadstr

Eekhoutstr

Eekhoutpoort

15

21

Nieuwe Gentweg

16

20

Willemijnendreef

3

33

Jacobinessenstr

Gentpoortstr

Gentpoortvest

4

Oude Gentweg

Boudewijn Ravestr

Gentpoortvest

Buiten Gentpoortvest

5

Visspaanstr

Senilllienhof

25

32

Katelijnestr

For more see

Top Experiences ⭐ p60
Experiences ⭐ p70
Eating 🍴 p74
Drinking 🍷 p75
Shopping 🛍 p76

Katelijnevest

N 0 ——— 200 m
0 ——— 0.1 miles

6

E **F** **G** **H**

59

⭐ **TOP EXPERIENCE**

Groeningemuseum

The Groeningemuseum *(visitbruges.be/en; adult/child €15/7)* is a candidate for Bruges' most celebrated art gallery. While not enormous, it packs in an astonishingly rich collection of Flemish Primitive and Renaissance works. There's an eye-popping Hieronymus Bosch and more meditative works by Jan Van Eyck and Hans Memling. Later artists featured include Fernand Khnopff, Magritte and Delvaux.

MAP P58 **D3**

PLANNING TIP
If you're short on time for your visit, focus on works by the Flemish Primitives, which are the high point of the museum.

Scan this QR code for opening hours and tickets.

Flemish Primitives

Things take off artistically in the Flemish Primitives room, titled 'Bruges, a thriving art metropolis', which is crammed with works by Jan Van Eyck, Rogier Van der Weyden and Gerard David. These pieces depict the conspicuous wealth of the city and its surrounding landscapes with glittering realistic artistry.

Typical examples include the *Madonna Crowned by Angels* (1482) by the Master of the Embroidered Foliage, where the rich fabric of the Madonna's robe meets the 'real' foliage at her feet with exquisite detail, and Van Eyck's *Madonna with Canon Van der Paele* (1436). Van Eyck's portraits, like those of his counterparts, reflect the abundance of the city in their time, while adding a further dimension of psychological realism. Rogier Van der Weyden's *St Luke Drawing the Madonna* features an ecstatic breastfeeding Jesus and gentle Madonna being sketched by the somewhat pained-looking Luke, the pin-sharp backdrop of watery Bruges draped with gorgeous towers and gables.

![Groeninge Museum interior]

GROENINGE MUSEUM © MUSEUMS OF BRUGES

Hans Memling, Jan Provoost & Gerard David

At the end of the 15th century Bruges was losing its financial mojo as Het Zwin, the waterway to the sea, began to silt up. But the city's artistic life was in full swing, attracting genius painters such as German Hans Memling; the white-clad virgin and angel in his *Annunciation* have a statue-like grace. Look on in awe at the way Memling painted folds of cloth. In the year Memling died, 1494, Jan Provoost came to town. Provoost became known for innovations such as presenting the crucifixion in a horizontal format; his semi-realistic semi-surreal *Death and the Miser* remains cryptic.

Bruges was still a key player in the city's art. Gerard David's grisly *Judgement of Cambyses* (1498) features the cityscape: it was designed for the town hall, and was intended to strike fear into those making unjust rulings.

QUICK BREAK
Fuel up with carrot cake, hot chocolate and other treats at attractive tearoom De Proeverie (p75), which is less than a five-minute walk from the gallery.

NOT SO PRIMITIVE
Fifteenth-century Bruges saw a group of groundbreaking painters who pioneered painting in oil on oak boards, adding thin layers of paint to produce bright colours and exquisite detail. They became known as the Flemish Primitives. But not all were Flemish and their work was anything but primitive: the name derives from the Latin *primus,* meaning first – an indication of their innovative and experimental approach.

Renaissance Bruges

Dutch painter Hieronymus Bosch is represented by a *Last Judgement,* where fantastical creatures run wild, and heaven looks just as bizarre as hell. Another *Last Judgement* is that of star Bruges painter Pieter Pourbus, whose work has echoes of Bosch's, and shows an awareness of Italian Renaissance painting. His marriage portrait of wine trader Jan van Eyewerve and Jacquemyne Buuck still gleams with the confidence and mercantile prosperity of the era. The Bosch-esque contraption with a windmill-based mechanism in the background of Jan's portrait is a crane, installed in the city in 1290.

From 1600, the Pourbus and Brueghel dynasties came to dominate the art scene. Pieter Brueghel II's *The Sermon of St John the Baptist* is one of the most attractive paintings in the gallery, with its focus on peasant life and engaging details: a red-stockinged man clings to a tree to better see John, and a dog sits patiently on his master's cloak.

Modernity

Genre paintings and neoclassicism dominate the next few rooms, with works that are dull compared with the innovative mastery of those in the preceding galleries. Things pick up artistically with Frank Brangwyn's *Canal in Bruges,* which hums with crepuscular mystery, and with the shrouded gloom of symbolist painters such as Henri Le Sidaner.

Works from the 1920s show the influence of cubism and German expressionism on Flemish artists – most striking are Constant Permeke's earth-coloured depictions of peasant life in *Pap Eaters* and *The Angelus.* Two further rooms also cover the modern period: there's a typically androgynous figure by superstar symbolist Fernand Khnopff, and the gallery closes with works from the '60s and '70s, which show the influence of arch-surrealist Magritte.

⭐ **TOP EXPERIENCE**

Museum Sint-Janshospitaal

In the restored chapel of a 12th-century hospital building, Museum Sint-Janshospitaal *(visitbruges.be/en; adult/child €15/7)* is best known for its Memling paintings and reliquary. Following a bold restoration, these and other paintings as well as artefacts from the hospital's long history are displayed alongside contemporary pieces.

MAP P58 **C4**

The Memling Paintings

A priceless collection of works by Hans Memling glow in the dim light of Museum Sint-Janshospitaal; Memling was born in Frankfurt, but spent most of his painting career in Bruges, and his fruitful association with Sint-Janshospitaal resulted in the commissioning of the glowing religious works now displayed here. The largest work is the triptych of *St John the Baptist and St John the Evangelist,* commissioned by the hospital church as an altarpiece. Look out for St Catherine (with spinning wheel) and St Barbara, both seated at the feet of the Virgin. Memling's secular portraits are just as engrossing as the devotional work, such as the delicate *Portrait of a Young Woman* (1480), where the subject's hands rest on the painted frame of her portrait.

The Reliquary of St Ursula

This gilded oak reliquary (pictured on p64) looks like a miniature Gothic cathedral. It was painted by Memling with scenes from the life of St Ursula, including highly realistic Cologne cityscapes, and counts among Bruges' most important treasures. The devout Ursula was a Breton princess betrothed to a pagan prince. She agreed to marry him on the

PLANNING TIP
The museum shop has excellent in-depth guides to the exhibits and paintings.

Scan this QR code to book tickets.

MUSEUM SINT-JANSHOSPITAAL © MUSEA BRUGGE

A QUICK BREAK
Head down Mariastraat until it turns into Katelijnestraat, and enjoy takeaway veggie offerings from De Bron (p75).

condition that she could make a pilgrimage to Rome (via Cologne) with 11,000 virgins. All were murdered on the return journey by the king of the Huns, along with Ursula and her betrothed.

Pick up one of the cards nearby and fold and draw or write on your own reliquary offering.

Sint-Janshospitaal Artefacts

Lofty Sint-Janshospitaal has been elegantly restored to show off both the exposed beams of the 12th-century building and an array of fascinating artefacts relating to the museum. The latter includes torturous-looking medical implements, hospital sedan chairs and a gruesome 1679 painting of an anatomy class. A marvellous 1778 artwork shows the hospital in action, very recognisably in the space where you are standing. The nuns serve food, lift a patient out of bed, and pray with the sick.

Don't miss the attic with its magnificent oak roof truss: one of the oldest in Europe. The 'Closer to Memling Experience' allows you to customise Memling's paintings – this is unlikely to improve them, but actually the large screens let visitors hone in on masterly details that might otherwise be missed.

Contemporary Art

Remarkably, Museum Sint-Janshospitaal is also now a contemporary gallery. Visitors can place their hands on a scarlet metal heart monitor on arrival, joining the heartbeats of everyone who has entered here. Neon artwork *Persona Grata* was created by Lahouari Bakir in 2023, inspired by the community's guidelines for hospitality written in 1188.

Berlinde De Bruyckere's fallen archangel is a crumple of feathers on a plinth with fragile legs emerging, and deeply moving video works muse on illness, death and mourning. In perhaps the most touching, a psychiatrist, counsellor and intensive care nurse/war survivor talk about homelessness, trauma and grief.

But the most striking piece is Patricia Piccinini's unlikely pieta. *The Bridge* features two figures made from silicone, fibreglass and human hair: a woman cradling a boar-like hybrid creature with immense care.

Pharmacy

Though it's not the main event, the 17th-century *apotheek* (pharmacy) is worth a look; it was in use till the early 1970s. It's a beautiful tiled space with rows of jars and a pendulum clock. Take a peek into the Trustees Room, adjoining the pharmacy, which is lined with portraits of bewigged and ruffled trustees. The four garden beds outside are a tiny remnant of the 3000-sq-metre garden, which the sister-apothecaries used to grow their herbs.

HANS MEMLING
Possibly trained in Brussels under van der Weyden, German-born Hans Memling (c 1440–94) arrived in Bruges aged around 25 and swiftly became a favourite among the city's merchant patrons. In 1465 he was granted citizenship of Bruges, and a 1480 tax document reveals he was one of the city's richest residents, in part due to his many fashionable portraits of donors, either individual portraits or incorporated into his large religious tableaux.

⭐ **TOP EXPERIENCE**

Gruuthusemuseum

Gorgeously restored in the last few years, the Gruuthusemuseum (*visitbruges.be; adult/child €15/7*) of applied arts is one of Bruges' must-sees. It features a romantic heraldic entrance in a courtyard of ivy-covered walls and dreamy spires: originally built in the 13th century, the building was transformed with Victorian Gothic panache.

MAP P58 **D3**

PLANNING TIP
Photographers should check out the views from the museum's balcony, artfully framed by stone arches. Look down at the little arched bridge for one of the most picturesque vistas in the city.

Scan this QR code to book tickets.

The Entrance Hall

Taking its name from the flower-and-herb mixture (*gruut*) that was used to flavour beer before the cultivation of hops, the Gruuthuse boasts a grandiose entrance hall, given over to a huge tapestry of wool and silk, depicting the liberal arts and weaving in Bruges in the 17th century.

Explore the Rooms

Beyond the entrance hall, the Gruuthuse comprises a marvellous warren of 17 rooms crammed with treasures, as well as a lofty studio. Room 1 features a portrait of original owner, Louis de Gruuthuse, wearing the Order of the Golden Fleece, as well as a fascinating 16th-century map of Bruges and a monumental 19th-century fireplace. Other treasures include the stained glass in room 3, illuminated manuscripts in room 4 and historic guild paraphernalia in room 11. In room 13 you'll find a superb collection of lace, from ruffs to collars to fans; frothy Mechelen lace adorns a man's white jacket, and portraits show the elaborate lace bonnets and shawls that well-to-do women wore in the late 18th century.

Seven Wonders

Don't miss *The Seven Wonders of the City of Bruges* painted by Pieter Claeissens I in 1550–76. Combining

© FEMKE DEN HOLLANDER

faithful landscape painting with a dash of Hierony-mus Bosch, it shows the marvels of the medieval city, not as they actually were, but in a mash-up where they adjoin each other. The wonders include the towers of the Church of Our Lady and the Belfry, the Waterhuis and the crane depicted in Pieter Pourbus' marriage portrait in the Groeningemuseum (p60).

The Oratory

The extraordinary oak-panelled oratory, or private chapel, was built in the 1470s for Louis de Gruuthuse and his wife Margaretha to eyeball Mass at Onze-Lieve-Vrouwekerk (p70): you can peek through a window in the oratory for a knock-out view of the church's Gothic chancel. Don't miss the carved angels that support the vaults of the ceiling, and the initials L and M.

QUICK BREAK
Stroll down a tranquil back street to delightful De Stoepa (p74), for bistro food and a pleasant hippie vibe.

WALKING TOUR

Parks & Gardens

This leafy route takes you from the fish market south and into some of Bruges' loveliest green spaces. Stroll through Koningin Astridpark, picking up a pastry at local favourite Schaeverbeke, then head into Minnewater round the Lake of Love. Stop off to visit the tranquil whitewashed begijnhof, then circle back to where you started.

START	END	LENGTH
Vismarkt	Vismarkt	3.4km; 2–3hr

EXPLORE

SOUTH BRUGES

1 Fishy Bruges

The handsome colonnaded 1821 **fish market** (Vismarkt; p54) is still open for business most days. Fishmongers have been selling their North Sea produce here for centuries, though these days only a few vendors set up on the cold stone slabs. Join locals buying snacks such as *maatjes* (herring fillets) or, if you're starting this walk in the afternoon, browse the craft stalls.

2 Park & Patisserie

Walk south along Jozef Suvéestraat for a few minutes until you reach local hang-out **Koningin Astridpark**, named for the Swedish wife of King Léopold of Belgium; you'll come across her bust when you reach the park. Walk through the park, pass the Gothic revival Magdalen Church and you'll reach the scrumptious Patisserie Schaeverbeke (p75) at Schaarstraat 2. Long a local favourite, it serves outstanding pastries and sourdough bread.

3 City Gateway

Continue south to **Gentpoort**, one of the town's four medieval gateways; it now houses a small local history museum. Look out for the niche housing a statue of St Adrian, who was thought to protect the city from the plague. From here, a pleasant footpath leads through the greenery along the water's edge.

4 The Lake of Love

Follow the path west until you reach **Minnewater** (p70) and its eponymous park, a scenic green space with orderly flower beds and secluded paths. Times have changed in Bruges: it's hard to believe that the serene waterway, known to locals as the 'Lake of Love', was once the city's inner harbour, where exotic cargoes of wool, wine, spices and silks were unloaded.

5 Look Out for the Horse's Head

Just north of the park, **Wijngaardplein**, a touristy but still irresistible square, is ringed by bar-cafes and features a horse-head fountain where the city's carriage horses are watered. The cafes here are a little on the pricey side, but the views are refreshing.

6 Beautiful Begijnhof

Over the little arched bridge from the square, the 13th-century **Begijnhof** (p70) is one of the delights of Bruges, its whitewashed buildings encircling a garden with tall trees and swathes of daffodils in spring.

From the Begijnhof, cross the water and head up Wijngaardstraat to turn left onto Katelijnestraat. Bear right onto Gruuthusestraat (which becomes Dijver) and head back to the Vismarkt.

EXPERIENCES

Walk on the Tranquil Side
NOTABLE BUILDING

Dating from the 13th century – it just celebrated its 800th anniversary – Bruges' **Begijnhof** (MAP: ❶ P58 **C5**; *visitbruges.be/en*) remains a remarkably tranquil haven, despite the hordes of summer tourists. In spring a carpet of daffodils adds to the quaintness of the scene. The last *begijn* has long passed away, but there is a convent of Benedictine nuns at the pretty whitewashed complex.

The baroque church of the Beguinage features a flamboyant high altar, 17th-century choir stalls and chubby cherubs adorning the choir screen. Outside, tall elm trees frame the view of the whitewashed houses, and despite the occasional crowds there's still a secluded, village-like air to the place.

Explore the Lake of Love
LAKE

Opposite the Begijnhof is the **Minnewater** (MAP: ❷ P58 **C6**) canal – known unofficially as the 'Lake of Love' – adjacent to a charming park of the same name. The romantic area has plenty of sheltered paths and benches to retreat to on a sunny day. In Bruges' medieval heyday, this is where ships from far and wide would unload their cargoes of wool, wine, spices and silks.

The Prettiest Bruges Bridge
PARK

Behind the Arentshuis, **Hof Arents** (MAP: ❸ P58 **D3**) is a charming little park with a humpbacked pedestrian bridge, Sint-Bonifaciusbrug, which crosses the canal and offers idyllic views. Nicknamed 'Lovers' Bridge', it's where many a Bruges citizen steals their first kiss. Privileged guests staying at the Guesthouse Nuit Blanche get the romantic moonlit scene all to themselves once the park has closed.

Holy Treasures
CHURCH

Dominating the surrounds, 13th-century **Onze-Lieve-Vrouwekerk** (MAP: ❹ P58 **C3**; *museabrugge.be/*

 BEGIJNHOVEN

In the 12th century, large numbers of men from the Low Countries embarked on crusades to the Holy Land and never returned. Many of their women-folk chose to become a *begijn*. These lay sisters made Catholic vows of obedience and chastity, but could maintain their private wealth. They lived in a self-contained *begijnhof:* a cluster of houses built around a central garden and church, surrounded by a protective wall. These all-female communities were self-sufficient. Most had a farm and vegetable garden and made supplementary income from lacemaking and from benefactors, who would pay the *begijnen* to pray for them.

en; museum adult/child €8/4) was reopened in 2015 after extensive renovations. Its enormous 115m spire is unmissable throughout much of the city. Inside, it's best known for Michelangelo's serenely contemplative *Madonna and Child* (1504) statue, the only such work by Michelangelo to leave Italy during the artist's lifetime. Look out also for the *Adoration of the Shepherds* (1574) by Pieter Pourbus.

In the church's apse, the treasury displays some splendid 15th- and 16th-century artworks, plus the fine stone-and-bronze tombs of Charles the Bold (Karel de Stoute) and his daughter, Mary of Burgundy, whose pivotal marriage dragged the Low Countries into the Habsburg Empire, with far-reaching consequences.

Beer Heaven
BREWERY

Founded in 1856, though there has been a brewery on the site since 1564, **Brouwerij De Halve Maan** (MAP: **5** P58 **C5**; *halvemaan.be; adult/child €16/8.50*) is the last family *brouwerij* (brewhouse) in central Bruges. Multilingual, 45-minute guided visits depart on the hour. These include a tasting but can sometimes be rather crowded. Alternatively, you can simply sip one of their excellent Brugse Zot (Bruges Fool, 7%) or Straffe Hendrik (Strong Henry, 9%) beers in the appealing brewery bar-cafe. In 2016 a 3km beer pipeline, leading to the bottling point, was installed

FREE BRUGES
Legends Walking Tours
A series of wildly popular (and free) guided walks (p48).

Onze-Lieve-Vrouwekerk
A must-visit for art lovers: sadly Michelangelo's sculpture can't be viewed for free, but the rest of the church can.

Begijnhof
Stroll the paths around its white-washed buildings and enjoy a deeply tranquil escape.

Coupure Canal
Swim for free, getting up close and personal to some watery city infrastructure (p72).

Minnewater
The park surrounding the 'Lake of Love' is a gorgeous spot for a picnic: pick up some affordable fare from a local supermarket.

Vismarkt
This fish market (p54) has operated since 1821 and is a great spot for people-watching and browsing the craft stalls.

under the brewery's cobbles; it's up to 34m below ground in parts.

Swim in a Canal
SWIM

If you're visiting the city in the warmer months, don't miss the glorious opportunity to swim in a Bruges canal. A section of the

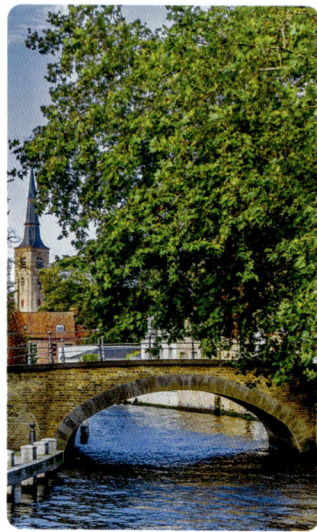

HARRY BEUGELINK/SHUTTERSTOCK

Bruges by Boat TOUR

The must-do activity in Bruges is to see the city by water on a 30-minute **canal-boat tour**. Boats depart roughly every 20 minutes from jetties south of Burg, including Rozenhoedkaai and Dijver. Each operator is essentially a branch of one or two companies regulated by the city: they all do the loop; they all cost the same.

Modern Art in an Ancient City ART CENTRE

Discover Bruges' contemporary concert hall, **Concertgebouw** (MAP: P58 **A4**), by way of superb sound and video installations roped together into the **Concertgebouw Circuit** (*concertgebouw.be; adult/child €12/6*). Allow two to three hours to fully explore this evolving collection – and to participate. You can activate steel tubes with your body to create music, tap a coloured dome to release a huge spectrum of sounds and, on the roof of the building, play carillon bells.

Coupure Canal (MAP: 6 P58 **F1**; pictured above) is roped off and a temporary pontoon installed: take a dip for free, with swans and canalboats passing in the distance. Lifeguards and cold showers are on hand.

🖼️ **MADONNA & CHILD**

Michelangelo's *Madonna and Child* is extraordinary in many ways, and not just for its masterful naturalism and grace. The sculpture was stolen from Bruges (and Belgium) twice. In 1794 it was shipped to Paris after French revolutionaries conquered the Austrian Netherlands (to which Bruges belonged at the time). Twenty-one years later, the Madonna was returned to Bruges after Napoleon's defeat at Waterloo. Then in 1944 retreating German soldiers smuggled the sculpture to Germany. A year later, it was discovered in a salt mine in Altaussee, Austria, which the Nazis used as a huge repository for stolen art – and thankfully returned to the Church of Our Lady. The Madonna's calm downcast gaze belies the drama of her history.

Theatre, classical music and dance performances are regularly staged. The tourist office is situated at street level.

Dodgy Diamonds

MUSEUM

While Antwerp is now the centre of the diamond industry, the idea of polishing the stones with diamond 'dust' was originally pioneered in Bruges. This is the theme of the slick **Diamantmuseum** (MAP: **8** P58 **D4**; *diamondmuseum.be; adult/child €12/8*), which also displays a lumpy, greenish 252-carat raw diamond and explains how the catchphrase 'diamonds are forever' started as a De Beers marketing campaign. The tone is celebratory, and the narrative skims a little too lightly over the racist, colonial history of diamond mining.

Triënnale Bruges

FESTIVAL

Bruges is reviving the art **Triënnale** (*triennalebrugge.be*) first held in the city in the late 1960s and early '70s, with themes ranging from reimaginings of sedate Bruges as a megapolis to the trauma beneath the skin of this dreamy destination. During past events, Brazilian artist Henrique Oliveira sculpted huge knotted wooden branches around ancient city walls in a tangled image of the subconscious mind, while Tunisian artist Nadia Kaabi-Linke's huge circular bench stuck with shining pins

FESTIVE BRUGES

Heilig-Bloedprocessie
On Ascension Day, Bruges' biggest folklore event (p43) sees the parading around town of an enormously revered reliquary supposedly containing a few drops of Christ's blood. For a grandstand seat book well ahead.

Cactus Music Festival
Indie pop and alternative **music festival** (*cactusfestival.be*) held in July in Minnewater Park.

Festival Musica Antiqua
This weeklong festival of **medieval music** (*mafestival.be*) takes place in Bruges in the first week of August, with recitals at the Concertgebouw.

Golden Tree Pageant
Every five years in mid to late August, Bruges lays on this grandiose **procession** (*goudenboomstoet.be*) celebrating the 1468 marriage of Charles the Bold to Margaret of York. Next on in 2028.

that actively prevented meetings symbolised exclusivity and elitism. The Triënnale Brugge in 2027 promises to once more integrate modern imaginings into the ancient streets, provoking visitors to think beyond tourist cliches.

Best Places for...

G Budget **GG** Midrange **GGG** Top End

See p58 for map of locations

Eating

Belgian Food

In 't Nieuwe Museum **GG**

 9 H2

Family-owned local favourite serving succulent meat cooked in a 17th-century open-fire oven. Specials include veggie burgers, eel dishes and *vispannetje* (fish casserole). *nieuw-museum.com; 6-11pm Fri, Sat, Mon & Tue, 12.30-2.30pm & 6-11pm Sun*

One Restaurant **GG**

10 D5

Excels in straightforward but tasty Flemish fare: shrimp croquettes, meatballs in cherry and beer sauce, and Flemish beef stew for mains, and flambéed apples for dessert. *onerestaurant. be; noon-2pm & 6-9pm Wed-Sun*

Resto Ganzespel **GG**

 11 G1

A truly intimate eating experience in a lovely old gabled building; the owner serves classic Belgian dishes such as meatballs and *kalfsblanket* (veal in a creamy sauce). *ganzespel. be; 6.30-10pm Sat & Sun*

Délice Brugge **GG**

12 D5

Located near the Minnewater Park, warm-hearted Délice dishes up Flemish beef stew, rabbit with potato croquettes, fresh mussels and other Belgian specialities. It's small and cosy: book ahead. *delicebrugge.be; 11am-9.30pm Thu-Tue*

'T walpoortje **GG**

13 D5

Stoofvlees (rich beef stew) and mussels with *frites* (fries) are the stars of the menu here, washed down with Trappist beer or Belgian wine. Exposed brick walls and gingham tablecloths give a homely feel. *11.30am-9pm Wed-Mon*

Bistro Food

De Stoepa **GG**

 14 B6

Bistro-style food is served in a hippie ambience, with beautiful statues and wooden floors and furniture all giving a homey but stylish feel. *stoepa. be; noon-2pm & 6pm-midnight*

Christophe **GG**

15 E3

A cool late-night bistro with marble tabletops and a decent range of Flemish staples, including fresh Zeebrugge shrimps. *christophe-brugge.be; 6pm-1am Thu-Mon*

Resto Mojo **G**

16 F3

Located near Koningin Astridpark, Mojo is a cosy bistro bar that serves finger food such as tapenades with ciabatta, and well-priced mains including cod goujons and moussaka. *restomojo.be/eng; 5-11pm Thu-Mon*

Fine Dining

In the Mood **GGG**

17 D6

An elegant eatery on the edge of Minnewater Park that dishes up classic Flemish dishes – plus outdoor Bar Boutique where you can quaff a cocktail. *moodfoodcafe .be/en; noon-2.30pm & 6-11.30pm*

LESS Eatery

18 **A3**

Three-star Michelin chef Gert de Mangeleer's sharing concept with Japanese style and unforgettable flavours. Sleek interior near the concert hall. *lesseatery.be; noon-2pm & 7-9.30pm Tue, Fri & Sat, 7-9.30pm Mon, Wed & Thu*

Cafes & Bakeries

De Proeverie

19 **C4**

A chintzy but appealing tearoom serving a variety of teas, gloopy hot chocolate, milkshakes plus crème brûlée, chocolate mousse and *merveilleux* cake. *deproeverie.be; 9.30am-6pm*

Patisserie Schaeverbeke

20 **F3**

This gorgeous patisserie has been around for 35 years, serving exquisite French pastries such as *cannelés de Bordeaux* and financiers, as well as artisanal bread. *7.30am-7pm Fri-Wed*

Yarn

21 **E3**

Stylish place with streetside seating and a courtyard garden that excels at brunch: try the fluffy pancakes with fruit or the next-level French toast. Lunch and dinner mains are beautifully presented. *8am-2pm Tue-Sun, 8am-2pm & 6-9pm Fri & Sat*

Carpe Diem

22 **D5**

Old-school Belgian bakery near the Beguinage with ornate wooden panelling and latticed windows. Settle in for excellent sandwiches, exquisitely pretty cakes and a good range of teas. *tearoom -carpediem.be/en; 7am-6pm Wed-Sun*

Quick Eats & Takeaway

Marco Polo Noodle Bar

23 **D4**

You can't beat this little noodle bar for its wide range of Asian flavours, from pho to ramen and dumplings, too. Great value. *marco-polo -noodles.com; noon-3.30pm & 5-9.30pm*

De Bron

24 **D5**

By the time this glass-roofed takeaway has its

doors open, there's a queue of diners keen to get vegetarian fare from *de bron* (the source). *11.45am-2pm Mon-Fri*

Mount Gorkha

25 **E6**

This little snack bar styles itself as a *frituur* (chip shop), but rather than chips order one of their flavourful Nepalese curry dishes. Excellent *momo* steamed dumplings, and you can have biryani spiced to order. *11.30am-2.30pm & 5-11pm Tue-Sun*

Drinking

Cafes/Pubs

't Klein Venetie

26 **E2**

Don't miss the superb canal view from outside this popular bar-cafe. Its view is lovely any time, but especially compelling at dusk as the floodlights come on. *kleinvenetie.be; noon-midnight*

L'Estaminet

27 **E2**

With dark-timber beams, convivial clatter and a park setting, L'Estaminet has hardly changed since it opened in 1900. Primarily a drinking spot, but it also serves time-honoured dishes such as spaghetti Bolognese with a cheese crust. *noon-late*

Bars & Live Music

The Vintage

 B4

Unusually hip for Bruges, with a 1960s/'70s vibe and a vintage Vespa hanging from the roof. The sunny terrace is a nice spot for a Jupiler, and the themed parties can be raucous. *facebook.com/thevintagebrugge; 11am-1am Thu-Tue*

Bieratelier

29 **D5**

Known for beer tastings, and with 12 options on draft, this is a friendly little bar decorated with thousands of beer mats. Soak up the brews with burgers and loaded fries. *bier-atelier.be; noon-11.30pm*

Cactus Muziekcentrum

 A3

The city's top venue for contemporary and world music, hosting live bands and international DJs. It also organises events including July's Cactus Music Festival. *cactusmusic.be; 5pm-late Thu-Sat*

Shopping

Local Crafts & Art

Sashuis

31 **C6**

This fantastical step-gabled building on Lake Minnewater has been repurposed for the Handmade in Brugge initiative, showcasing Bruges' craftspeople. *handmadeinbrugge.be/sashuis-en; 11am-6pm Wed-Sat*

Simbolik

32 **E6**

Studio/workshop open in spring and summer, with candles, cards and artworks decorated in wonderfully distinctive calligraphic script. *simbolik.be; 9.30am-2pm Mon-Wed, to 6pm Fri & Sat*

Galerie Broes

33 **E4**

This beautiful Bruges building contains an elegant and highly personal fine art gallery, a world away from nearby trinket stalls. *broes.be; 10am-noon & 1.30-6pm Tue-Sat*

Ginkgo

34 **C5**

A shop and workshop, where the owner custom makes silver jewellery, with nature-inspired designs including gingko-leaf pendant earrings. *yourginkgojewels.com; 11am-6pm Mon-Sat*

Silver Hand

35 **G1**

Make your own jewellery at silver-ring or wedding-ring workshops; it uses recycled silver, and you can choose your finish and add an engraved message. *silverhandworkshop.com*

Food & Drink

Sukerbuyc

36 **D4**

One of the tastiest chocolate shops in the city, run by a third-generation chocolatier who uses fresh ingredients and no preservatives. *sukerbuyc.be; 10am-6pm Tue-Sun*

Oud Huis Deman

37 **H1**

A mother and daughter bakery that has been going for an incredible 150 years: lovingly crafted treats include Bruges rusks cooked from a 135-year-old recipe, crispy lace cookies and strips of scrumptious almond bread. look out for their products across town. *oudhuisdeman.be/en*

Kaashuys Den Hof
38 E2

Try before you buy at this excellent cheese shop with an array of Flemish cheeses: there are even some Bruges-specific varieties. *kaashuysdenhof.be; 9am-6.30pm Tue-Sat, to 1pm Sun*

Comics & Books

De Striep
39 D4

Look for Thibaut Vandorselaer's wonderful illustrated guides at this colourful comic shop. There's also a collection of comics and graphic novels in Dutch, French and English. Bruges-based comics are by the counter.

striepclub.be; 10am-7pm Tue-Sat, 2-6pm Sun

Brugse Boekhandel
40 D2

Book-lovers' heaven (pictured above), with titles in English as well as Flemish and French. Lace lovers look out for their array of titles on the craft. *brugseboekhandel.be/en; 9am-6.30pm Mon-Sat*

Explore Brussels

Triumphal arch, Parc du Cinquantenaire (p136)
JORISVO/SHUTTERSTOCK

See p102
for eating,
drinking and
shopping
listings

Explore
The Grand-Place
& Îlot Sacré

Researched by Mélissa Monaco

Brussels' heart beats in the Grand-Place. Just walking on its cobblestones, ringed by gold-trimmed gabled houses (built by merchant guilds) and flanked by the 15th-century Gothic town hall, you'll find it hard to disagree with Jean Cocteau that this is the most beautiful theatre in the world. In the 12th century, the square was used as a marketplace – the names of the surrounding lanes still evoke herbs, cheese and poultry. Nearby are glass-covered shopping arcades and Brussels icon Manneken Pis. Plus, don't forget that Brussels is a city that appreciates the finer things in life: restaurants, bars and cafes abound.

Getting Around

 Metro
The fastest way to travel. Gare Centrale/Centraal Station and De Brouckère on line 1 and 5 serve this neighbourhood.

 Tram
Practical for those coming by international train or bus. Lines 4 and 10 connect the centre with Gare du Midi and Gare du Nord. Get off at Bourse/Beurs or De Brouckère.

 Bus
If you're staying outside of the city centre, buses are very convenient. Buses 71 and 29 stop at De Brouckère, bus 95 at Grand-Place.

THE BEST

ARCHITECTURAL JEWEL
Grand-Place (p84)

ICON
Manneken Pis (p88)

PALACE
Galeries Royales Saint-Hubert (p94)

BELGIAN COMICS
Centre Belge de la Bande Dessinée (p90)

BEER HEAVEN
Moeder Lambic Fontainas (p104)

Hôtel de Ville (City Hall), Grand-Place (p84)
CATARINA BELOVA/SHUTTERSTOCK

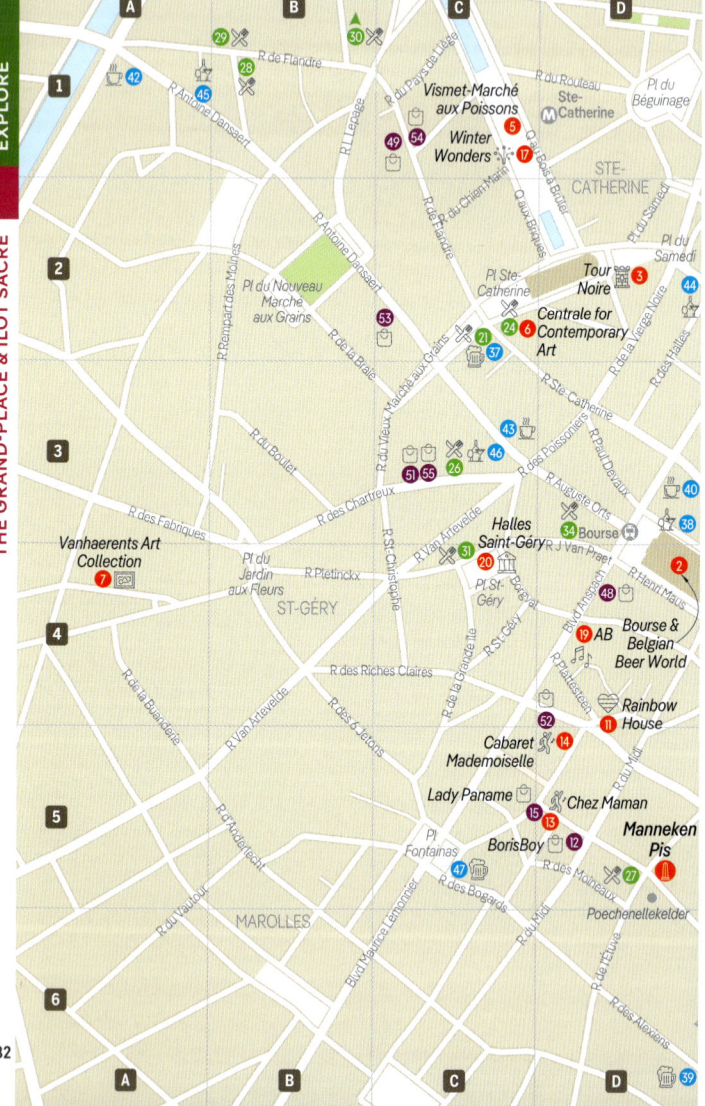

A B C D

1

29
42
28
45
R de Flandre
30
R du Pays de Liège
R Antoine Dansaert
R L'Eperon
Vismet-Marché
aux Poissons
R du Rouleau
Pl du
Béguinage
49 54
Winter
Wonders
5
Ste-
Catherine
17
STE-
CATHERINE

2
R Antoine Dansaert
Remparts des Moines
Pl du Nouveau
Marché
aux Grains
R de la Braie
R du Flandre
R du Chien Marin
Quai Bois à Brûler
R aux Choux
53
Pl Ste-
Catherine
21
37
Tour
Noire
3
Pl du
Samedi
Centrale for
Contemporary
Art
24 6
R de la Vierge Noire
44
R des Halles

3
R au Boulet
R des Fabriques
R des Chartreux
R du Vieux Marché aux Grains
43
26
46
R des Poissonniers
R Paul Devaux
R Ste-Catherine
R Auguste Orts
51 55
40
38

Vanhaerents Art
Collection
7
Pl du
Jardin
aux Fleurs
R St-Christophe
R Plétinckx
ST-GÉRY
R Van Artevelde
Halles
Saint-Géry
31
20
34 Bourse
R J Van Praet
48
2
R Henri Maus

4
R de la Blanchisserie
R Van Artevelde
R de la Grande Île
R des Riches Claires
R des 6 Jetons
Pl St-
Géry
R St-Géry
Bd Anspach
R Plattesteen
19 AB
Bourse &
Belgian
Beer World

Rainbow
House
52 14
11
Cabaret
Mademoiselle

5
R Anderlecht
Lady Paname
15 13
BorisBoy
Chez Maman
12
Manneken
Pis
Pl
Fontainas
47
R des Bogards
R des Moineaux
27
Poechenellekelder

6
R du Vautour
MAROLLES
Bd Maurice Lemonnier
R du Midi
R des Alexiens

82

A B C D
39

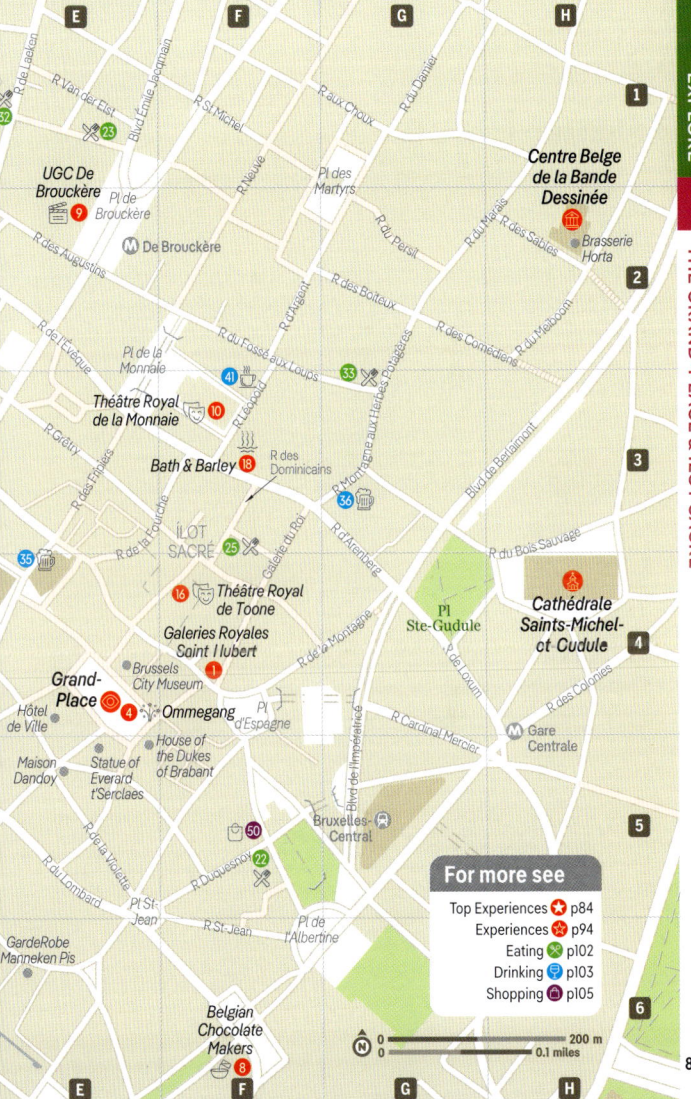

E F G H

1

R de Laeken
R Van der Elst
Blvd Émile Jacqmain
R St-Michel
R aux Choux
R du Damier

**Centre Belge
de la Bande
Dessinée**

32

23

UGC De
Brouckère

Pl de
Brouckère

9

M De Brouckère

R des Augustins

R aux Choux
Pl des
Martyrs
R Neuve
R du Persil
R des Marais
R des Sables
Brasserie
Horta

2

R de l'Évêque

Pl de la
Monnaie

R du Fossé aux Loups

R des Boiteux
R des Comédiens
R du Meiboom

41

33

R Gréty
R des Fripiers

**Théâtre Royal
de la Monnaie**

10

R Léopold

R Montagne aux Herbes Potagères

R des Comédiens

3

Bath & Barley 18

R des
Dominicains

36

Blvd de Berlaimont

R de la Fourche

35

ÎLOT
SACRÉ

25

Galerie du Roi

R d'Arenberg

R du Bois Sauvage

16

**Théâtre Royal
de Toone**

Galeries Royales
Saint Hubert

1

Pl
Ste-Gudule

**Cathédrale
Saints-Michel-
et-Gudule**

4

**Grand-
Place**

4

Brussels
City Museum

Ommegang

House of
the Dukes
of Brabant

Pl
d'Espagne

R de la Montagne

R de Loxum

R Cardinal Mercier

R des Colonies

M Gare
Centrale

Hôtel
de Ville

Maison
Dandoy

Statue of
Everard
t'Serclaes

Blvd de l'Impératrice

Bruxelles-
Central

Gare
Centrale

5

R de la Violette

50

R Duquesnoy

22

R du Lombard

Pl St-
Jean

R St-Jean

Pl de
l'Albertine

6

GardeRobe
Manneken Pis

**Belgian
Chocolate
Makers**

8

For more see

Top Experiences ⭐ p84
Experiences 🌟 p94
Eating ❌ p102
Drinking 💧 p103
Shopping 🛍 p105

N 0 ——————— 200 m
   0 ——————— 0.1 miles

E F G H

★ TOP EXPERIENCE

Grand-Place

Brussels' Grand-Place stuns with its towering 15th-century Hôtel de Ville (City Hall) and its antique guildhalls (mostly 1697–1705), all trying to outdo each other with fine baroque gables, gilded statues and elaborate guild symbols. It's simply one of the world's most beautiful UNESCO heritage sites.

MAP P82 **E4**

QUICK BREAK
Take time out for *speculoos* biscuits, tea and ice cream at historic **Maison Dandoy** (*maisondandoy. com*) just off the Grand-Place.

Scan this QR code for Hôtel de Ville's opening hours and tickets.

Hôtel de Ville

Built between 1444 and 1480, the splendid Hôtel de Ville was almost the only building on the Grand-Place to escape the 1695 French bombardment. The creamy stone facade is covered with Gothic gargoyles and reliefs. On top of the soaringly tall tower is a gilded statue of St Michael, the patron saint of Brussels. Now that city officials have relocated to their new offices at BruCity, the city hall is fully open to visitors. Highlights include the Gothic Hall, the Marriage Hall – where weddings are still celebrated, and newlyweds can wave from the balcony – and the mayor's former office, decorated with paintings of a bygone Brussels when the Senne river flowed through the city. If you're not afraid of heights, the city hall organises a weekend tour to the top of the spire.

Houses & Guildhalls

Each of the Grand-Place's gorgeous buildings and guildhalls (pictured right) are worth taking a moment to look at. Here are some of the most important, listed by street number and guild.

Le Roy d'Espagne (No 1; Bakers) is decorated with a bust of Charles II, King of Spain and monarch of the Southern Lowlands – that's

SHEVCHENKO ANDREY/SHUTTERSTOCK

present-day Belgium. At **La Louve** (No 5; Archers), look up for the golden phoenix rising from the ashes, which signifies the rebirth of the house, which was destroyed three times (the last time was during the 1695 French bombardment). **Le Cornet** (No 6; Boatmen) has, fittingly, a stern-shaped gable. Its name is a call to the horn on its facade. At **Le Cygne** (No 9; Butchers), admire the carved swan above the door. It used to be a cafe and hosted Karl Marx in 1847. Ironically, it now houses upscale private events. **L'Arbre d'Or** (No 10; Brewers) features hop plants climbing the columns. If you're interested, it hosts the **House of Belgian Brewers** and its small museum. **Le Pigeon** (No 26–27; Painters; look for its namesake above the door) was home to French writer Victor Hugo when the author of *Les Misérables* was living in exile in Brussels.

PLANNING TIP
Free tours always start on the Grand-Place, offered by multiple companies. Get maps and information at the Visit Brussels' branch located in the Hôtel de Ville.

HISTORY

The Grand-Place began as a medieval marketplace. In the 15th century, guilds built their guildhouses around it, mostly in wood. In 1695, when in conflict with the League of Augsburg, French troops bombarded the city, destroying most buildings on the Grand-Place. Rebuilt in just a few years, even better than before, in a stunning baroque style, it's a testament to Brussels' resilience.

House of the Dukes of Brabant

Occupying the whole southeastern side of the square, this **mansion** consists of seven houses from 1698, located behind a single palatial facade that was reworked in 1882. Had the imperial governor had his way after 1695, the whole square would have been built in the same palatial style. It owes its name to the busts of the dukes and duchesses of Brabant placed atop the pilasters. Spot the Windmill House, home to Victor Hugo in 1852 before he moved on to the Pigeon House. No 15 (La Fortune) hosts the only hotel located on the Grand-Place: Hôtel Résidence Le Quinze.

Maison du Roi

This fanciful feast of neo-Gothic arches, verdigris statues and mini spires is bigger, darker and nearly 200 years younger than the surrounding guildhalls. Built on the site of a former bread market, the current masterpiece dates from 1873 and houses the **Brussels City Museum** (brusselscitymuseum. brussels), which features old maps, architectural relics and paintings. Don't miss Pieter Brueghel the Elder's 1567 *Cortège de Noces* (Wedding Procession), and the real statue of Manneken Pis (the one at the fountain is a copy).

Statue of Everard t'Serclaes

This 1902 **statue** of city hero Everard t'Serclaes depicts his reclining dying body, after being attacked by the henchmen of Sweder van Abcoude, the Sire of Gaasbeek, in a dark tale of land appropriation. An enraged population raised a small army to lay siege to the castle of Gaasbeek, bringing many chickens as provisions, earning the Bruxellois their nickname of *kiekefretters* (chicken eaters). A fairly contemporary 'tradition' claims that rubbing the arm of the statue will bring you good luck.

★ **TOP EXPERIENCE**

Cathédrale Saints-Michel-et-Gudule

Perched on top of the Treurenberg hill, this impressive Catholic cathedral is the most significant religious building in Belgium. Host to coronations and royal weddings, the Gothic masterpiece, with its twin towers, reminded a homesick Victor Hugo of Paris' Notre-Dame.

Cathedral Art

Stained-glass windows flood the soaring nave with light. The prettiest are in the north and south transepts representing Charles V and his wife, Isabella, and his sister, Mary of Hungary, with her husband. Both were designed based on drawings by famous Renaissance painter Bernard van Orley. Rows of apostles brandish gilded tools while an enormous wooden pulpit by Antwerp artist Hendrik Verbruggen sees Adam and Eve expelled from Eden by skeletons. The cathedral is also the resting place of several historical figures such as the archduke Albert and archduchess Isabel, and Austrian Netherlands governor Charles of Lorraine.

Visit the Crypt & Climb the Towers

Built on the site of an earlier church dedicated to St Michael, construction of the cathedral began in 1226 and lasted 300 years. The church also housed the remains of St Gudula, an 11th-century noblewoman known for her pious life. Both saints are patrons of Brussels. The cathedral is a beautiful example of Brabantine Gothic architecture, characterised by its two massive towers and elements of flamboyant Gothic style. Visitors can access the crypt and treasury for a small fee. To climb the cathedral towers (€10; Saturday from March to October with guided tour), sign up two weeks in advance.

MAP P82 **H4**

PLANNING TIP
The wheelchair-accessible entrance is located on the right side of the cathedral. Get in touch before your visit, as the doors are usually locked.

Scan this QR code for opening hours and tour bookings

★ **TOP EXPERIENCE**

Manneken Pis

On the corner of Rue de l'Etuve and Rue du Chêne stands Brussels' most famous citizen in all his innocent nakedness, peeing for the world to see, a perpetual grin on his face. Is it a smile of relief or provocation? Probably both.

MAP P82 **D5**

QUICK BREAK
Despite the touristy location, **Poechenelle-kelder** (henellekelder .be/en) is a great place to sample traditional Belgian beers. Manneken Pis Café (p102) makes the best *carbonnades* (stewed beef) in town.

Scan this QR code for the GardeRobe's opening hours and tickets.

The Origins

The little boy's origins are somewhat murky, but there's a mention of a statue of a boy peeing water to feed a public fountain as early as 1452. This was not the statue we see today; in 1659 a bronze sculpture by Jérôme Duquesnoy the Elder replaced the original. By 1770 Manneken Pis was moved to its current location and received new decorative elements, transitioning from a public facility to an ornamental piece. The statue has been stolen and damaged numerous times, requiring two complete restorations. The original was finally moved to the Maison du Roi while a copy carries on the duty of amusing visitors and keeping the free spirit of Brussels alive.

Legends of Manneken Pis

Several legends surround the fountain's existence. One story tells of a boy who saved the city by urinating on a wick to extinguish a fuse leading to bombs placed by an enemy. Another involves a lad who urinated on a witch's door and was turned into a statue when caught. The most historically accurate would be the story of Duke Godfrey III of Leuven, whose father died when he was a toddler. In 1142 the two-year-old lord's troops fought

SAVVAPANF PHOTO/SHUTTERSTOCK

against rebellious lords. To boost the soldiers' morale, the infant duke was placed in a basket and hung from a large oak tree above the battlefield. As his men struggled, the little duke stood up in the basket and urinated on the field, the sight of which galvanised his troops to win the day.

GardeRobe Manneken Pis

'Little Julien', Manneken Pis' given name, owns a wardrobe of more than 1100 costumes, and it's growing by the years. A festival, event or dignitary's visit is always an occasion to bestow a new outfit. The **museum** displays 150 outfits, the oldest one being a gentleman's costume gifted by French King Louis XV as a gesture of apology for the theft of the statue by his army's soldiers.

PLANNING TIP
Buying a ticket to visit the Brussels City Museum includes entrance to the GardeRobe Manneken Pis.

Centre Belge de la Bande Dessinée

Belgium's comic strip centre takes you through the evolution of comics: how they're made, seminal artists and their creations, and contemporary comic-strip artists. Even if you're not particularly interested in comics, at least take a look at Victor Horta's 1906 light-filled glass-and-steel textile warehouse in which the museum is housed.

MAP P82 **H2**

PLANNING TIP
You don't have to pay an entry fee to visit the central hallway or to drink a coffee at the attached cafe, Brasserie Horta.

Scan this QR code to book tickets

The Invention of the Comic Strip

The history of the ninth art goes right back to antiquity and makes a compelling case that the manuscripts of medieval monks – with their divided story strips and speech bubbles – were the first cartoon strips. The revolution continues through to the picture stories of 19th-century New York newspapers.

The Museum of the Imagination

This gallery focuses on Belgium's favourite cartoon character – Tintin – created by the great Hergé. He posits Tintin as a visually blank 'everyman' who can transform himself into a granny, a turbaned Indian or a white-bearded sage. Volatile Captain Haddock is, by contrast, a volcano of uncontrolled emotion, while the narrative is often sparked by the misunderstandings and bizarre actions of Professor Calculus. Among other Belgian artists – explored in less depth – you may want to pause over the little blue creatures created by Peyo: the Smurfs. Both Tintin and the Smurfs represent the two major schools of Belgian comics. The Brussels school, with Hergé as a guiding figure, favoured the *ligne claire* (clear line) style characterised by strong lines and colours. The Marcinelle school, centred around the Dupuis publishing house, is often referred to as 'the big nose school' due to its cartoonish characters,

MICHAEL MULKENS/SHUTTERSTOCK

with the Smurfs being a prime example. Both schools had rival magazines: *Le Journal de Tintin* for the Brussels school, and *Le Journal de Spirou* (named after a famous character) for the Marcinelle school, the latter still being published today.

Note: the top floor of the museum highlights the works and creative processes of famous international comic strip artists.

Horta's Building

Designed as a department store in 1906, this lovely building features a swirling tiled floor, slim metal pillars, girders and grills, and light filtered through a glass ceiling. As you enter, to the right is a small exhibition about the construction, decline (in 1965, when the department store closed) and restoration of the building (between 1987 and 1989).

QUICK BREAK
The adjoining cafe, **Brasserie Horta** (*brasseriehorta. be*), is an attractive place that serves Belgian standards such as *frites* (fries) and shrimp croquettes.

WALKING TOUR

Dansaert & Sainte-Catherine

Cosy and hip at the same time, the twin neighbourhoods of
Dansaert and Sainte-Catherine are also full of history: atmospheric
Sainte-Catherine was the heart of Brussels' former harbour; Rue
Dansaert, built in the 19th century, is lined with stately buildings
and home to high-end, mostly local fashion stores.

START	END	LENGTH
Isabelle Bajart	Place Sainte-Catherine	1.5km; 1hr 45min

THE GRAND-PLACE & ÎLOT SACRÉ

EXPLORE

1 Fit for Carrie Bradshaw

Fancy **Isabelle Bajart** (p105) is one of Brussels' most carefully curated vintage stores. Some of the garments are collectors' items: you'll find shoes, as well as leather purses, evening dresses... Just nearby, check out Flash Capsule (p105) concept store and grab a coffee to go.

2 Hidden Bookshop

Tucked down a passageway, **Passa Porta** *(passaportabookshop.be)* bookshop is well worth a look with its strong, literary-focused English-language selection. It's a great stop for meeting people, as there are regular literary events held here. Passa Porta also supports and hosts writers in exile.

3 Belgian Style

Stijl (p105) is the showcase for long-established but still edgy Antwerp designers, such as Ann Demeulemeester and Dries Van Noten. Don't be shy, the shop is more welcoming than it looks. The women's store is at Rue Dansaert 74 and the men's store, almost opposite, on Place du Nouveau Marché aux Grains 6.

4 Simply Delightful

Go take a peek at **Rue de la Cigogne**, a miraculously preserved medieval narrow street lined with tiny houses with climbing plants and wisteria dangling above your head.

5 Beer Stop

Sample old Brussels when you are in need of some refreshment at **Au Laboureur** *(aulaboureur.be)*. In the morning and afternoon, see the elderly ladies and gentlemen come for a coffee or a game of cards before the terrace gets filled with a younger, ubercool crowd.

6 Sustainable Presents

Plants in a bottle, no-waste cosmetics, colouring books, tea... **Urban Therapy** (p105) offers its own products alongside a selection from other creators who meet their sustainability standards.

7 Old Harbour

You've reached the **Vismet-Marché aux Poissons** (p96), Brussels' former fish market. Once a series of docks linked to the Senne and Willebroek Canal, the basins were filled in the 19th century under Mayor Anspach. A fountain added in the 1970s honours him; its female figure represents the Senne, resting in her tunnel. It originally stood on Place de Brouckère.

8 Fishy Ending

The village-like Place Sainte-Catherine is filled with restaurants. Once the salt wharf, it's now presided over by the 'new' Sainte-Catherine Church built in the 19th century (only the baroque bell tower of the old church remains). It's time to have shrimp croquettes at **Mer du Nord** (p102)!

EXPERIENCES

Shop & Gawk at Galeries Saint-Hubert
SHOPPING

When opened in 1847 by King Léopold I, the glorious **Galeries Royales Saint-Hubert** (MAP: ❶ P82 **F4**; pictured right; *grsh.be*) formed Europe's very first shopping arcade. Many enticing shops lay behind its neoclassical glassed-in arches, flanked by marble pilasters. Several eclectic bar-cafes spill tables onto the gallery terrace, safe from rain beneath the glass roof. The arcade is off Rue du Marché aux Herbes, close to the Grand-Place. Among the stores present, you'll find many upscale chocolatiers; you can't really go wrong here. If you'd like to sample different chocolates from different makers, ask for them by the piece. Some stores will require a minimum number of pralines to purchase but it will allow you to try a variety of flavours and artisanship.

Learn about Brewing at Belgian Beer World
MUSEUM

The Bourse is Belgium's 1873 stock exchange building and is the location of the new museum, **Bourse & Belgian Beer World** (MAP: ❷ P82 **D4**; *belgianbeerworld. be; adult/student €19/16*). After enjoying its grandiose neoclassical facade, come inside the covered passageway and admire the soaring and ornate rotunda. The four caryatids are the work of Auguste Rodin, then a young apprentice sculptor. Make your way to the 1st floor for your introduction to Belgium's pride and joy: beer. First, learn about beer culture and its importance in the Belgian psyche, followed by an explanation of the brewing process (with many interactive features to make things fun). After an hour and a half, beer-making will no longer hold any secrets. A tasting at the rooftop bar **Beerlab** (*thebeerlabrooftop.be*) is a perfect finish with 150 brews to choose from. Being so close to the statues at the top of the stock exchange will make you feel closer to heaven. Plus, you don't need a ticket to visit the bar.

 CHANGE OF DESTINY

Facing away from Sainte-Catherine Church, look right. The well-preserved houses (numbers 3 to 7) once belonged to the Protestant Church. In 1878, at number 5, a red-headed Dutchman attended classes at the 'Flemish training college for evangelists and pedlars'. After he'd failed religious studies in Amsterdam, his family sent him to Brussels, where the education was considered 'a bit more relaxed'. His name was Vincent van Gogh, and he only lasted three months. Although he later became an evangelist in one of Belgium's poorest areas, he soon turned to art. The rest is history.

VITALII VITLEO/SHUTTERSTOCK

Look for the Medieval First Wall
HISTORIC SIGHT

Experts are unsure when Brussels' first defensive wall was built but estimate it was in the 12th century. Two centuries later, it already proved obsolete, and a new wall was built. A few remnants of the first wall and its towers remain and finding them makes for a nice walk through the historical Brussels.

Start with the **Tour Noire** (MAP: ③ P82 D2), behind the Sainte-Catherine Church. Restored in the 19th century, it's literally 'embraced' by two aisles of the Novotel hotel. At Rue des Chartreux 42, peek inside the Demarteau clock repair shop to see a piece of the wall. The most evocative remains are **Courtine and Tour de Villers** with a large piece of curtain wall and a squat tower. Further along, the tall Anneessens tower stands along the busy Blvd de l'Empereur. This tower is named after François Anneessens (1660–1719), the head of the Four Crowns guild. He was imprisoned for treason by the Austrian regime and subsequently decapitated in the Grand-Place.

Go Back in Time with the Ommegang
FESTIVAL

In 1549 Charles V's empire, including present-day Belgium and the Netherlands, was at its height. Tired of ruling, he considered abdicating in favour of his son, Philip. who was born and raised in Spain and in contrast to his father, who was born in Ghent, did not know this part of his empire. Charles decided to take Philip to Brussels to be 'introduced' and on the occasion, the magistrate of the city threw him a lavish procession whose magnificence is well documented in writing and painting: the **Ommegang** (MAP: ④ P82 **E4**). Originally a religious procession dedicated to Our Lady of Victories, *ommegang* means 'going around', as the procession followed a loop. Revived in 1930 after being banned during the French Revolution, the UNESCO-listed event now sees thousands reenact the historical procession each July, culminating in a Grand-Place show with flag throwers, horsemanship demonstrations, jousts and more.

Chill at the Vismet   SQUARE

When the sun comes out (perhaps for a total of two weeks a year, as Belgians like to joke), people flock outdoors to cure their chronic vitamin D deficiency by making the most of the city's many terraces.

The hotspot in the city centre is undoubtedly the **Vismet-Marché aux Poissons** (MAP: ⑤ P82 **C1**; pictured right), the old fish market. Once the site of the former harbour, this vast public space – with its two ornamental ponds – is now lined with restaurants and bars. One of the simplest pleasures in life is grabbing food and drinks to go, sitting beside the pools in the sunshine, and enjoying the afternoon and evening in a relaxed, friendly atmosphere, often shared with a younger crowd.

Pursue Contemporary Art at Centrale   ART

True, Belgium is known for its Flemish masters, but that doesn't mean the artistic scene is stuck in the past; quite the contrary. The contemporary art scene is particularly vibrant in Brussels. **Centrale for Contemporary Art** (MAP: ⑥ P82 **C2**; *centrale. brussels*) is the city's art exhibition hall. Located inside an industrial building (Brussels' first power plant), it focuses on emerging talents and hosts young artists in residence. The plant in itself has quite a story and its loft spaces are almost as

 SNOW GLOBE HOUSE

The door at number 46 Rue de Flandre may look like any other front door, but it hides a secret. If that door is open, step inside, ask the desk attendant if it's OK to go on, walk through the corridor and glass doors, and discover La Bellone. This 18th-century house turned cultural institution and its courtyard are encased in glass, like a house in a snow globe. Pop in to take a peek at this unique space, or attend an event or a meeting with the artists in residence: La Bellone is dedicated to the performing arts.

ALIAKSANDR ANTANOVICH/SHUTTERSTOCK

interesting as the works of art it hosts. It was built in almost the exact place as the former Ste-Catherine Church, whose entrance was Rue Sainte-Catherine, around the corner. Deemed too unsound to be renovated, the church was destroyed and the power plant, and its office, were built in its place. The baroque bell tower, next to the new church built in the 19th century, is the only part left standing.

Marvel at the Vanhaerents Art Collection   ART

At the edge of the Dansaert neighbourhood, find the **Vanhaerents Art Collection** (MAP: **7** P82 **A4**; *vanhaerentsartcollection.com;*

adult/youth €12/6), the work of several decades by real-estate magnate Walter Vanhaerents and his children. Considered the most prestigious private art collection in Belgium, pieces by Ai Weiwei or Jeff Koons rub shoulders with South American, African and African American artists in a 1926 former warehouse. The gallery is only open once a month and needs to be booked in advance. Visit the website to check the schedule.

Become a Chocolatier at Belgian Chocolate Makers   WORKSHOP

Belgium, along with Switzerland, is a country that takes chocolate very seriously. If you've ever wondered how

97

Belgians have mastered the craft of chocolate-making and wished to try creating chocolate bonbons yourself, why not book a workshop with **Belgian Chocolate Makers** (MAP: **8** P82 **F6**; *shop.chocolaterie.brussels*)? During this hour-and-a-half session, certified chocolatiers Elisabetta and Patricia will share everything you need to know about chocolate, from tasting cocoa beans to sampling various types of chocolate from different origins. They will demonstrate how chocolate is crafted, and then it's your turn to unleash your creativity by making your own *mendiants* (round chocolates decorated with nuts and dried fruits), truffles and chocolate bars. The groups are small, allowing the chocolatiers to provide personalised attention to each participant's needs and questions.

Catch a Film in Style   CINEMA

After WWII, Brussels was filled with grand cinemas: the Marivaux, the Métropole, the Mirano and the Agora are names older locals still recall with a sparkle in their eyes. Most had closed by the early 1990s, although some survived. The most beautiful theatre still standing is the Grand Eldorado, inside the **UGC De Brouckère** (MAP: **9** P82 **E2**). Built in 1932 by architect Marcel Chabot, its largest room was restored in 1992 to its former glory: exotic Art Deco gilded reliefs by artists Wolf and Van Neste depict scenes from daily life in colonial-era Congo. Above the screen, an enormous sun seems to set, as if ready to make way for the film. If there's a blockbuster playing, it's bound to be here.

Spend a Night at La Monnaie Opera   CLASSICAL MUSIC

Théâtre Royal de la Monnaie (MAP: **10** P82 **F3**) is not just an opera house: it's where the Belgian Revolution began in 1830. During a performance of *La Muette de Portici*, Belgian patriots – frustrated after years of being ruled by the king of the Netherlands and following Napoleon's defeat at Waterloo – were roused by

---

 HOW BELGIUM BECAME INDEPENDENT

Belgium became independent in 1830 after a revolution against Dutch rule. Following Napoleon's defeat in 1815, the Congress of Vienna had merged the Protestant Dutch north and Catholic Belgian south into one kingdom. Tensions quickly rose due to cultural, religious and economic differences. On 25 August 1830 the performance of *La Muette de Portici* at Brussels' opera house sparked riots that turned into a full-scale uprising. After weeks of conflict, Belgian revolutionaries declared independence. The major European powers recognised Belgium as a neutral state in 1831, and Leopold I became the nation's first king on 21 July of that year.

the aria *Amour Sacré de la Patrie* (Sacred Love of the Fatherland). Riots broke out, and after a short revolution, Belgium became independent. Today, La Monnaie ranks among Europe's top opera venues, renowned for the quality of its programme, musicians and singers. Every season includes classics (2026 will feature *Falstaff*, *Norma* and *Tosca*), contemporary creations and concerts. The Italian-style main hall is breathtaking – draped in red, shimmering with gold, and crowned by a grand fresco covering the entire rotunda. You might even spot the king and queen in their royal box! Can't attend a show? La Monnaie and its workshops are open for guided visits on Saturdays.

Follow the Rainbow to the Rainbow Village
LGBTIQA+

Belgium is known as one of the most LGBTIQA-friendly countries in Europe. Just a stone's throw from Manneken Pis, rainbow-coloured sidewalks guide you to the charming Saint-Jacques neighbourhood, a vibrant meeting point for the community. The compact area between Rue du Lombard, Platesteen and Rue du Marché au Charbon – nicknamed the Rainbow Village – is packed with bars, cabarets, a fetish shop, a love shop and, at its heart, **Rainbow House** (MAP: **11** P82 **D4**). This community centre brings together various LGBTIQA+ associations and offers a welcoming

ENTERTAINMENT & QUIRKS IN THE RAINBOW VILLAGE

BorisBoy
The largest **shop** (MAP: **12** P82 **D5**) for gay men. Leather and club wear, fetishist items, underwear, toys and much more.

Chez Maman
Historic drag show **cabaret** (MAP: **13** P82 **D5**). The legendary Maman may have passed the torch to Sugar Love but her spirit lives on!

Cabaret Mademoiselle
Decadent **cabaret** (MAP: **14** P82 **D5**) with drag performances, burlesque, magic show, musical acts... Its very own La Veuve was runner-up in *Drag Race Belgium*.

Lady Paname
Don't be shy and push the door of this boudoir-like **erotica/adult store** (MAP: **15** P82 **C5**). Lady Paname (aka Chantal) and her team will warmly welcome you and listen to your needs and wants.

in-house bar that may feel less intimidating than some of the wilder spots nearby. Historically, many venues have catered primarily to gay men, but all are welcome. Some spots are more about cruising, others are fetish-focused, and many are just great for music or a relaxed drink. Whatever your vibe, you're bound to find your crowd here.

Watch a Traditional Puppet Show

PUPPET SHOW

Eight generations of Toones have staged classic puppet productions in the Bruxellois dialects (the French and Dutch ones) at the **Théâtre Royal de Toone** (MAP: **16** P82 **F4**), a highlight of any visit to Brussels. Shows are aimed at adults, but kids love them, too. Puppetry has deep roots in the city: the art form started to thrive under Philip II of Spain, who shut down theatres fearing unrest due to the Spanish Inquisition, pushing locals to create clandestine puppet shows that became the 'people's theatre'. The tradition faded in the 20th century and Toone is the last survivor. Today, Nicolas Géal (aka Toone VIII) keeps both the free-spirited legacy and the dialect alive, staging witty, playful performances that mix history with humour. Tucked away at the end of a narrow impasse, Toone occupies a beautifully atmospheric 1696 house. Even if you don't come for a show, you can stop at the bar-cafe for a drink surrounded by *poechenelles* (puppets).

Celebrate the Holidays at Winter Wonders

FESTIVAL

As the holidays near, Brussels brightens the season's long nights with **Winter Wonders** (MAP: **17** P82 **C1**; pictured right), a sprawling Christmas market across the historic centre. Wooden chalets sell festive treats, mulled wine, gifts and artisan crafts (look for authenticity logos). The Vismet hosts the largest market with Ferris wheel views; Place de Brouckère adds an ice rink; while Place de la Bourse welcomes the yearly guest of honour. The Grand-Place dazzles with a sound-and-light show, while Sainte-Catherine's Québec Village tempts with poutine, maple syrup and music.

Have a Beer Spa Day

SPA

Only in Belgium can beer and wellness mix. At **Bath & Barley** (MAP: **18** P82 **F3**), kick things off by picking your hops to whip up a scrub. Then slide into a bubbling oak tub spiked with hops and herbs, with beer in hand (you can refill). Some packages add a sauna, but don't miss the finale: a nap on a straw bed. Quirky? Absolutely. Relaxing? Even more so.

THE VANISHING RIVER

The Senne (Zenne in Dutch) once flowed through the heart of Brussels, giving the city a look not unlike Bruges in old photos and paintings. Its polluted waters and overcrowded banks led to repeated cholera outbreaks, prompting Mayor Jules Anspach to tunnel and cover the river with grand boulevards crossing the city from north to south. The works, a major urban overhaul, lasted from 1865 to 1871. By 1955 the river was diverted outside the city, and its former tunnel repurposed for tram lines. The next time you ride lines 4 or 10, spare a thought for the lost river.

Rock Out at Ancienne Belgique

CONCERT

Right in the historic centre of Brussels, l'Ancienne Belgique (Old Belgium), now known as **AB** (MAP:  19 P82 **D4**), is the stuff of musical legend. Originally a music hall, this concert venue is now considered one of the best in Europe for its acoustics and intimate setting: it fits 2000 spectators on its floor and several balconies. The best and greatest have performed here – Jacques Brel, of course, but also David Bowie, Leonard Cohen, Lou Reed, Iggy Pop. The Cure famously fought on stage during their show here and briefly split up as a result. Always on the lookout for fresh talent, AB also has a smaller venue, **The Club**, offering a more relaxed atmosphere.

WERNER LEROOY/SHUTTERSTOCK

Have a Drink in Place Saint-Géry

BARS

It's hard to imagine that Place Saint-Géry, now surrounded by bars on every side, was once an island. In fact, it's where Brussels was born. This island, nestled between two arms of the Senne river, was home to the Saint-Géry Church – one of the first buildings to establish Brussels as a proper town. The remains of St Gudula, one of the city's patron saints, were kept here before being moved to the cathedral. The church was destroyed by French revolutionar-

ies and the area was turned into a market square. After Belgium's independence, the river also vanished – tunnelled underground as part of a grand plan to modernise the capital of the young nation. In 1881 a market hall, the Halles Saint-Géry, was built over the central fountain and its obelisk. Today, it houses an atmospheric bar-cafe beneath a soaring glass roof with elegant ironwork, and the **Halles Saint-Géry** (MAP: 20 P82 **C4**; *hallessaintgery.be*) also serves as a free exhibition space. There are plans to bring the market back in 2026.

LISTINGS

Best Places for...

G Budget **GG** Midrange **GGG** Top End

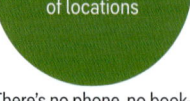
See p82 for map of locations

Eating

On the Cheap

Chouke **G**
21 C2
Have the best *frites* in the city centre at this no-frills *frituur* (chip shop). Don't miss the homemade burgers. *@fritkotChouke; noon-11pm*

Tonton Garby **G**
22 F5
Cheese-loving brothers serve custom sandwiches worth the wait, mixing veggies, fruits, sauces... They will literally interview you to know what you like. Friendly, chatty service. *11am-5pm Mon-Sat*

Super Fourchette **G**
23 E1
Vinyl shop meets cafe-canteen with homemade, seasonal, veggie-centric dishes and a chill vibe. Grab a record while your plate's cooking. *superfourchette. be; noon-2pm & 6.30-9.30pm Mon-Fri*

Belgian Classics

Mer du Nord **G**
24 C2
Enjoy your shrimp croquettes at this outdoor eatery by a fishmonger's window. Place your order, take a seat on the cobblestone square and wait for your name to be called. *noordzeemerdunord.be; 11am-6.30pm Tue-Sun*

Bouillon Bruxelles **GG**
25 F3
The tradition of Parisian bouillon has landed in Brussels! *Belle époque*–style eatery serving generous Belgian classics (*stoemp*, mussels, *américain*) at low prices. Full of charm and run by waitstaff in crisp uniforms. *bouillonbruxelles. com; 6-10.30pm Mon, noon-2pm & 6-10.30pm Tue-Thu, noon-3pm & 6-10.30pm Fri-Sun*

Fin de Siècle **GG**
26 C3
From *carbonade* (beer-based hotpot) and *kriek* (cherry beer) rabbit to moussaka and tandoori chicken, the food is as eclectic as the decor in this low-lit cult place.

There's no phone, no bookings, but the customers keep coming. *findesiecle. be; noon-midnight*

Manneken Pis Café **GG**
27 D5
Touristy location, but what looks like an old-fashioned *bruin café* hides a restaurant on the upper floor that makes the best *carbonades* in town. Kitchen closed on Monday. *mannekenpiscafe.com; hours vary*

Contemporary Cuisine

Kline **GG**
28 B1
In a raw, minimalist space (brutalist, the owner would say), Kline serves seasonal, locally sourced, but globally inspired, small plates (think crisp asparagus with miso). *kline.brussels; 6pm-midnight Tue-Sat*

Nightshop **GG**
29 B1
In a former garage, enjoy global, spontaneous cuisine and natural wines. The brainchild of former Londoner Jocasta Allwood is often full; book ahead. *@nightshop.*

brussels; 5-11pm Thu,
noon-11pm Fri & Sat

Fine Dining

Barge
30 B1

With its raw brick-and-wood decor, this spot mirrors Grégoire Gillard's seasonal, nature-driven cuisine. Request a seat by the open kitchen and watch the chef and his team preparing their colourful, tasty and perfectly balanced dishes: a high-flying act! *bargerestaurant.be; noon-2pm & 7-11pm Fri, 7-11pm Tue-Thu & Sat*

Entropy
31 C4

Elliott Van de Velde's restaurant serves a creative, gourmet six-course plant-based dinner and surprising organic wines. Profits support Hearth Project, his initiative against food waste and social inequality. *entropyrestaurant.be; noon-2.30pm & 7.30-11pm Fri, 7.30-11pm Wed, Thu & Sat*

International & Food Courts

Toukoul
32 E1

A fully immersive Ethiopian restaurant, where dishes are best shared and eaten with pancake-like injera: a

place to visit in a group rather than solo. Entertainment by musicians while you dine. *toukoul.be; noon-3pm & 6-11pm Sat & Sun, 6-11pm Mon-Fri*

Wolf
33 G3

Large (and often noisy) food court set in a former Art Deco–style bank. The space is stunning, and the wide choice of food, from savoury to sweet, should satisfy everyone. A tad expensive. *wolf.be; noon-10pm*

Yi Chan
34 D3

A modest and friendly family-run Sino-Vietnamese restaurant and (excellent) cocktail bar, decked out with an arch of plastic cherry blossom. The homemade dim sum hits the spot every time. *yichanbrussels.com; hours vary*

Drinking

Traditional Pubs & Historic Cafes

À la Bécasse
35 E4

Tucked down a narrow alley, À la Bécasse has communal tables and a

Brueghel-like vibe. Since 1877 it's served lambic beers – sour, non-fizzy, distinctly Brussels, and not for everyone. The drinks are a bit pricey. *alabecasse.com; 11am-midnight, to 1am Fri & Sat*

À la Mort Subite
36 G3

A timeless classic since 1928, with lined-up wooden tables, mirror panels and entertainingly brusque service. Great assortment of *gueuzes* and *krieks* (typical lambic-based beer from Brussels), and don't miss the cottage cheese tartines. *alamortsubite.com; 11am-11pm Mon-Sat*

Billie
37 C2

Dark wood, mirrors and opal lights set the mood of this classic Belgian pub. Mostly attended by Flemish locals, Billie serves a wide array of draught and bottled beers (and spaghetti in a second room). *billie.brussels; 11am-midnight Mon-Wed, to 1am Thu & Fri, noon-1am Sat, 2pm-midnight Sun*

Le Cirio
38 D3

This 1886 grand bar-cafe dazzles with polished brasswork and aproned waiters, while coiffured *mesdames* with small dogs dilute the gaggles of tourists. The house speciality is a half-and-half mix of still and sparkling wines. *lecirio. be; 10am-midnight*

La Fleur en Papier Doré
 39 **D6**

Once the haunt of Magritte and other artists, La Fleur still bears their souvenirs on its nicotine-stained walls. Grab a seat and enjoy the vibe of this real piece of Brussels culture. *lafleurenpapierdore.be; 10am-midnight*

Breakfast & Coffee Spots

Corica
 40 **D3**

With 175 years in the coffee-roasting business, Corica knows what it's doing with precious, single-origin beans, some of them rare (Jamaican Blue Mountains, Australian Skybury or La Réunion's Bourbon Pointu). A place for connoisseurs. *corica.be; 8am-6pm Mon-Fri, 10am-6pm Sat*

Frank
41 **F3**

The original Frank (there's another one

at Place Stéphanie) is located by La Monnaie. Its large, white room is crowned with a huge stained-glass light fixture. Classy! Delicious coffees, teas and Australian-style all-day breakfast. *frank.brussels; 8am-4pm Mon-Fri, 9.30am-4pm Sat & Sun*

MOK
 42 **A1**

MOK serves some of the capital's best coffee and offers a wide range of vegetarian-inspired recipes. A big picture window looks out onto Rue Dansaert. *mokcoffee. be; 8am-6pm Tue-Fri, 10am-6pm Sat-Mon*

Kage
43 **C3**

If you're into green tea, Kage is heaven: Japanese and Chinese brews, lattes and pastries in a mint-green minimalist space that turns into a cocktail bar on weekends, serving tea-infused concoctions, of course. *kagetea.be; 10am-6pm Sun-Thu, 10am-6pm & 7-11pm Fri & Sat*

Beers & Cocktails

58 Rooftop&Eatery
 44 **D2**

Splendid city views from the 9th floor of the city's administrative building.

No purchase required for just checking the view. *58.brussels; hours vary*

Life is Beautiful
45 **A1**

Sip gourmet craft cocktails, carefully prepared by Harouna and his team in an unpretentious atmosphere. *libcocktailbar.com; 6pm-midnight Thu-Sat, to 1am Fri & Sat*

L'Archiduc
46 **C3**

Ring the doorbell and step into the 1930s in this iconic cocktail bar/jazz lounge. Order the signature pisco sour and enjoy. The atmosphere heats up as the music switches to contemporary as the hours go by. *archiduc.net; 4pm-5am*

Moeder Lambic Fontainas
47 **C5**

For discerning beer aficionados: an ever-changing list of craft beers on tap, and by the bottle. Contemporary decor rather than old world with bare brick walls and booths backed with concrete. *moederlambic.com; 4pm-midnight Mon-Thu, noon-1am Fri & Sat, to 11pm Sun*

Shopping

Really Local Souvenirs

Brüsel
48 D4

Chic comic-book shop named after a book by one of Belgium's best-known contemporary comic artists, François Schuiten. Comics with English translations are available as well as figurines. *10.30am-6.30pm Mon-Sat, from noon Sun*

D'EN Belge
49 C1

Tiny shop chock-full of rare beers (mostly *gueuzes*, the local Brussels beer) but also Belgian wines and gourmet snacks and treats. Not sure what you're looking for? The friendly owner's here to help. *noon-7.30pm*

Manneke
50 F5

Not your average souvenir shop: bags, T-shirts, postcards, decoration items, jewels, books and food products, all made in Brussels or the vicinity. *11am-6pm Mon-Wed, to 6.30pm Thu & Fri, 10am-7pm Sat, 10.30am-6pm Sun*

Beauty & Style

Isabelle Bajart
51 C3

Isabelle takes great pride in curating the clothes and accessories that come into her vintage store. There are big names to be found (such as Yves Saint-Laurent) and some luxury items, as well as more affordable pieces. *noon-7pm Mon & Tue, 11am-7pm Wed-Sat*

Smell Stories
52 D4

Exclusive, craft perfumes and affordable samples and discovery boxes fight for the counter spaces while owners Kurt and Stéphane will take the time to find the scent you're looking for. *10.30am-6.30pm Wed-Sat*

Stijl
53 C2

A top address for women and men, Stijl is stocked with Antwerp Six designer ware (Ann Demeulemeester, Dries Van Noten) but also features up-to-the-minute designers. It's a hip place but not pretentious, and unlike in similar boutiques, prices are clearly labelled. *10.30am-6.30pm Mon-Sat*

Concept Stores

Urban Therapy
54 C1

This concept store brings together global makers with one key requirement: sustainability. Alongside Urban Therapy's own wellness line, find everything from peanut butter to books, candles, handbags and toys. *10.30am-7pm*

Flash Capsule
55 C3

This cute concept store combines local and/or handcrafted items from 80 different makers (ceramics, clothes, cosmetics, prints...) and a cafe, ideal for breakfast, light brunch or an afternoon break. Make sure to explore every corner of the shop. *11am-7pm Wed-Sat, noon-6pm Sun*

Chocolates

Galeries Royales Saint-Hubert
see 1 F4

Look no further, the best mainstream brands are here: Marcolini and his jewel-like chocolates; Neuhaus, inventor of the praline (chocolate-filled bonbon); Mary, a favourite for classics; and Corné Port-Royal, best for quality/price. *grsh.be; hours vary*

See p122 for eating, drinking and shopping listings

Explore
Royal Quarter

Researched by
Mélissa Monaco

The majestic Royal Quarter encompasses the Palais Royal de Bruxelles, the Palais de Justice and the Mont des Arts, which houses the city's premier museums in splendid buildings, all just steps apart. Around Place du Grand Sablon, you'll find antique shops, tearooms and chocolate boutiques while the Marolles still retains its working-class grit, despite rampant gentrification. Overlooking the Marolles, as if a warning to its inhabitants to behave, looms the Palais de Justice, a building of monstrous size, still covered in scaffolding after 40 years of renovation. Graceful churches and the elegant Parc de Bruxelles add to the area's rarefied air.

Getting Around

 Bus

Buses 33, 71 and 95 pass through the district.

 Metro

Porte de Namur station is the handiest for the place du Sablon while Louise is best for the Marolles with direct access to the elevator going down to the neighbourhood. Gare Centrale is best for Mont des Arts.

 Tram

No 92 runs along Rue Royale and Rue de la Régence, between the Parc de Bruxelles to the Palais de Justice.

THE BEST

FLAMBOYANT GOTHIC
Église Notre-Dame au Sablon (p115)

ART HISTORY
Musées Royaux des Beaux-Arts (p110)

GREEN RESPITE
Parc de Bruxelles (p118)

LUXE CHOCOLATE
Pierre Marcolini (p120)

MONSTER BUILDING
Palais de Justice (p119)

Église Notre-Dame au Sablon (p115)

D.BOND/SHUTTERSTOCK

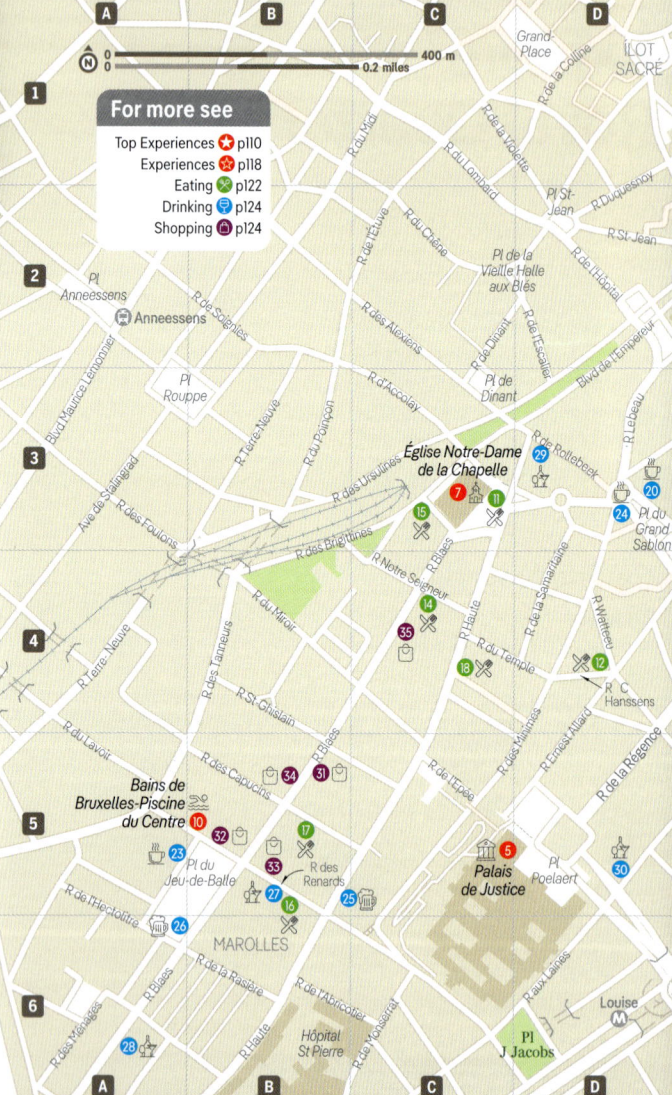

For more see

Top Experiences ⭐ p110
Experiences ❂ p118
Eating ❌ p122
Drinking 🅿 p124
Shopping 🛍 p124

Pl Anneessens

Anneessens

Pl Rouppe

Église Notre-Dame de la Chapelle

Pl de la Vieille Halle aux Blés

Pl de Dinant

Pl du Grand Sablon

Bains de Bruxelles-Piscine du Centre

Pl du Jeu-de-Balle

R des Renards

MAROLLES

Palais de Justice

Pl Poelaert

Hôpital St Pierre

Pl J Jacobs

Louise

Grand Place

ÎLOT SACRÉ

Pl St-Jean

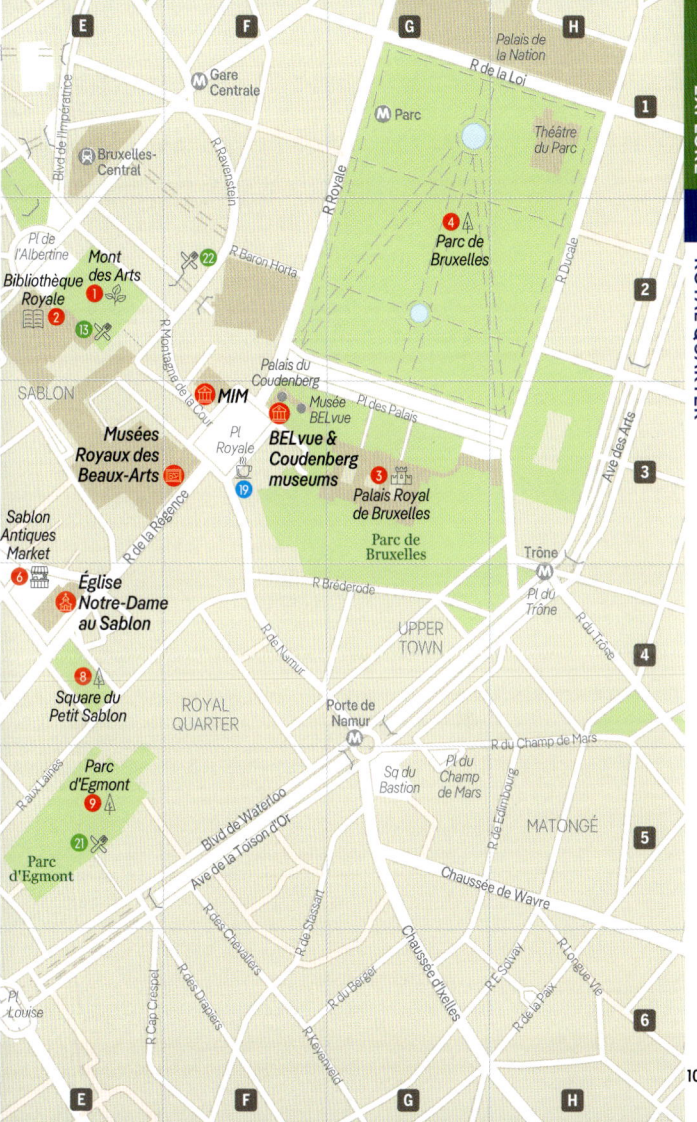

E
F
G
H

1
2
3
4
5
6

Palais de
la Nation

R de la Loi

Gare
Centrale

Bruxelles-
Central

Théâtre
du Parc

Pl de
l'Albertine

Bibliothèque
Royale

Mont
des Arts

R Ravenstein

R Royale

Parc

R Baron Horta

4
Parc de
Bruxelles

R Ducale

Ave des Arts

SABLON

R Montagne de la Cour

MIM

Palais du
Coudenberg

Musée
BELvue

Pl des Palais

Musées
Royaux des
Beaux-Arts

Pl
Royale

BELvue &
Coudenberg
museums

3
Palais Royal
de Bruxelles

Trône

Sablon
Antiques
Market

R de la Régence

6

Église
Notre-Dame
au Sablon

Parc de
Bruxelles

Pl du
Trône

R du Trône

R Bréderode

R de Namur

UPPER
TOWN

8

Square du
Petit Sablon

ROYAL
QUARTER

Porte de
Namur

R du Champ de Mars

Parc
d'Egmont

9

R aux Laines

Sq du
Bastion

Pl du
Champ
de Mars

R d'Edimbourg

MATONGÉ

21

Parc
d'Egmont

Blvd de Waterloo

Ave de la Toison d'Or

Chaussée de Wavre

Pl
Louise

R Cap Crespel

R des Drapiers

R des Chevaliers

R de Stassart

R du Berger

Chaussée d'Ixelles

R Keyenveld

R E Solvay

R Longue Vie

R de la Paix

109

Musées Royaux des Beaux-Arts

This prestigious museum incorporates the Musée Old Masters, in which the 15th-century Flemish Primitives are wonderfully represented; the Musée Fin-de-Siècle, focusing on art from 1868 to 1914 (closed for renovation); and the purpose-built Musée Magritte, the world's largest collection of works by the surrealist master.

MAP P108 **F3**

PLANNING TIP
Consider visiting Musée Magritte separately, as it merits at least two hours. A combo ticket lets you return later. Don't miss the sculpture garden, to the left facing the museum.

Scan this QR code for opening hours and tickets.

Flemish Primitives

These 15th-century masters are wonderfully represented in the gallery: search for Rogier Van der Weyden's *Pietà* with its strange dawn sky; Hans Memling's *Martyrdom of St Sebastian,* where a languid, almost ecstatic Sebastian is being pierced by arrows; Dieric Bouts' dramatic tableau depicting the torments of an unjustly accused husband and his faithful wife in *Justice of the Emperor Otto;* and the delicate *Madonna with Saints* by the anonymous artist known as the Master of the Legend of St Lucy.

The Brueghels

While Pieter the Elder was the greatest of this family of artists, the work of his sons, Pieter the Younger and Jan, also echoed his humorous and tender scenes, where the central narrative of the painting often has to be sought out among a wealth of lively, rustic details. If Pieter the Younger stuck to his father's favourite themes and style, Jan excelled in soft, colour-rich painting and rendition of flowers, earning him the nickname of 'Velver Brueghel'. The most famous example of Pieter the Elder's masterpieces is *Landscape with the Fall of Icarus,* where the hero's legs, disappearing into the waves, are

RADIOKAFKA/SHUTTERSTOCK

overshadowed by an unconcerned ploughman and a jaunty ship. Also not to be missed is *The Fall of the Rebel Angels*, where hellish creatures seemed to have come out from a substance-induced nightmare while a golden-armoured St Michael strikes the apocalyptic Beast, and angels swoop in serenely to join the fight.

Rubens & His Followers

Antwerp painter Pieter Paul Rubens specialised in fleshy religious works (*Massacre of the Innocents* or the delicate *Madonna with a Periwinkle*), and there are several colossal examples here. He was also fond of painting mythological subjects (the sensual *Jupiter and Semele*). However, his lesser-known works, such as *Four Studies of the Head of a Moor,* reveal his mastery of psychological portraiture. His second

QUICK BREAK
The museum cafe is a pricey but pleasant spot serving sandwiches, salads and cakes. Alternatively, walk to Place du Sablon for lunch or cake at the lovely Café Costermans (p123).

wife and muse, Helene Fourment, often inspired the master, and one of her many portraits graces the gallery. This section also features contemplative human studies by Anthony Van Dyck, a charming family portrait by Cornelius De Vos, and works by Rembrandt and Frans Hals.

More Recent Works

The Modern Art section of the museum has remained closed for several years; however, works from this collection are gradually being reintroduced into the Old Masters galleries. The newly established Léon Spilliaert Room, dedicated to works on paper, presents the symbolist artist's pieces – primarily executed on paper – in conversation with those of other artists during temporary exhibitions. Salle 54, also newly opened, features recent acquisitions of Belgian and international contemporary artists.

Musée Magritte

The adjoining Magritte museum offers a chronological exploration of the artist's work, including surreal and playful photos and films. Start from the top floor, making your way to the bottom, as his works are arranged in chronological order and by theme. In his famous canvases, motifs of spheres, pipes and birds appear repeatedly, as does the image of his wife Georgette. But before he found his 'signature', Magritte had a constructivist and futuristic period, which is often overlooked but nonetheless noteworthy. Visitors also can discover his works as an advertisement illustrator – and his movies.

★ **TOP EXPERIENCE**

MIM (Musée des Instruments de Musique)

The Art Nouveau Old England building is as much a highlight as the contents of MIM *(mim.be)* itself. This former department store was built in 1899 by Paul Saintenoy. Get your audio guide at the welcome desk and be ready to discover musical instruments in all their shapes and forms.

MAP P108 **F3**

Western Music History

This gallery contains a precious collection of Western wind, string and keyboard instruments; each instrument is numbered according to a point on the audio guide soundtrack you hear. The early variations on pianos, painted with delicate flowers and pastoral scenes, are among the most attractive items on display; also look out for the huge serpent-headed bassoons. The keyboard gallery digs a little deeper into the importance of these types of instruments and their influence on Western music.

Traditional Instruments

This gallery contains every instrument you've ever heard of, and then some. You can appreciate the aesthetic qualities of instruments from around the world as well as – via headphones – musical mastery, from the intricacies of the Indian sitar, the otherworldly wail of Tibetan horns to Congolese drums and harps.

Mechanical Music

The basement room is dedicated to mechanical instruments. Sounds range from a 16th-century church bell chiming midnight to a 19th-century bird organ and 20th-century hammond organ blues. Among the artefacts displayed is a barrel organ with wooden figures, which, when animated, enact some grisly teeth-pulling operations.

PLANNING TIP
The audio guide offers different tours (for children, peculiar instruments etc). Allow a minimum of two hours for the complete tour.

Scan this QR code for upcoming concerts.

★ TOP EXPERIENCE

BELvue & Coudenberg Museums

Right next to the Royal Palace, the Musée BELvue and Palais du Coudenberg are a two-for-one time-travel deal. The BELvue dives into Belgium's story since its independence, while the Coudenberg takes you underground into the ruins of the former palace of the Dukes of Brabant.

MAP P108 **F3**

PLANNING TIP
We recommend starting with the Palais du Coudenberg (minimum 45 minutes), followed by the BELvue (allow 1½ hours). Find a welcome coffee kiosk and terrace in the courtyard.

Scan this QR code to book tickets to Musée BELvue.

Musée BELvue

Take a tour through the airy stuccoed interior of this former royal residence *(belvue.be)* to explore Belgium's history from independence to today, brought to life by exhibits and film footage. The exhibit is divided into seven themes: democracy, prosperity, solidarity, pluralism, migration, languages and Europe. A gallery also showcases various Belgian inventions; you may be surprised by what this small country has contributed to the world, and you'll get to understand how this complicated little country works somehow.

Note: the museum is free on Wednesday afternoon.

Palais du Coudenberg

Coudenberg Hill (now Place Royale; *coudenberg. brussels*) was the site of Brussels' original 12th-century castle. Over several centuries, the castle was transformed into one of Europe's most elegant and powerful palaces, most notably as the 16th-century residence of Holy Roman Emperor Charles V. Around the palace, courtiers and nobles built their fine mansions. The vast complex was destroyed in a catastrophic fire in 1731, but beneath street level is the basic structure of the palace's long-hidden lower storeys. Meander along the ruins of the palace chapel and the great Aula Magna, and step on the ancient cobblestones of Rue Isabelle, a small street that was miraculously preserved.

⭐ **TOP EXPERIENCE**

Église Notre-Dame au Sablon

If you ask a local which Brussels church is the loveliest, chances are Église Notre-Dame des Victoires au Sablon (Onze-Lieve-Vrouw ter Zavelkerk) will come first. This fanciful Gothic jewel has been attracting pilgrims and miracle-seekers since the 14th century.

MAP P108 **E4**

The Stolen Madonna

The Sablon's large, flamboyantly Gothic church started life as the 1304 archers' guild chapel. A century later, it had to be massively enlarged to cope with the droves of pilgrims attracted by the supposed healing powers of its Madonna statue. The statue was procured in 1348 by means of an audacious theft from an Antwerp church – apparently by a vision-motivated husband-and-wife team in a rowing boat. The statue has long since gone, but a boat behind the pulpit commemorates the curious affair.

Interior

If the exterior is an intricate work of 'stone lace' and ogival windows, the interior is equally rich in decoration. Of particular interest are the stained-glass windows, most of which date from the 19th and early 20th centuries, gifted by wealthy patrons after the church underwent major renovations. The baroque St Ursula side chapel, decorated in black and white marble, is the final resting place of 15 members of the Tour et Taxis family, who oversaw the postal services since Burgundian times. The baroque wooden pulpit and the 18th-century great organ are also noteworthy.

PLANNING TIP
Entrance is free. For the best experience, visit mid-morning or late afternoon, when sunlight enhances the details of the stained-glass windows.

Scan this QR code to learn more about the Sablon church.

🚶 WALKING TOUR

Walk the Marolles

This partially gentrified working-class area is known for its colourful dialect and down-to-earth watering holes. To appreciate the Marolles' roots, head to Place du Jeu-de-Balle's morning flea market or pop into one of the neighbourhood bars; the crumbling brick chimneys are another remnant of the area's industrial past.

START	END	LENGTH
Gare de Bruxelles-Midi	Friture de la Chapelle	2.1km; 2hr

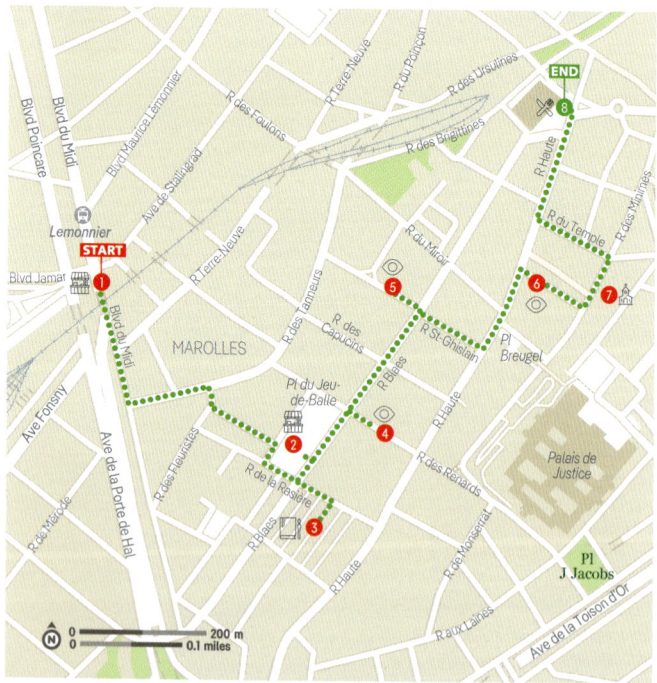

1 Multicultural Market

It's Sunday? Head from the Gare du Bruxelles-Midi to the **Marché du Midi**, said to be the biggest in Europe. This sprawl of colourful stalls next to the railway lines has an international flavour, with North African and Mediterranean spices, food, clothing and leather goods.

2 Old Market Bargains

Haggle at this popular, chaotic daily **flea market** *(9am–2pm)* on Place du Jeu-de-Balle. The best bargains are to be found early on weekday mornings. Secondhand books and clothes, vintage furniture and old cameras – you'll be surprised at what you can find. Stop for a coffee at the quirky Chaff (p124) on the northwest corner of the square – or have a full breakfast.

3 Art Nouveau Apartments

Almost hidden next to Place du Jeu-de-Balle, **Cité Hellemans** is a complex of Art Nouveau–style apartment blocks (1915). It's one of the first examples of this type of public housing in Brussels, and thoroughly photogenic.

4 Traces of Old Marolles

Narrow **Rue des Renards** exemplifies how the area is changing – on the right, heading downhill, are galleries, indie and vintage shops, and antique stores; on the left, cottages and traditional restaurants. You may come across vestiges of the old Marolles here, such as

vendors selling little pots of snails from their carts.

5 Horta Building

The lovely **Jardin d'Enfants** is the only school that Horta ever designed. As it's still a fully functioning school, you'll only be able to view it from the outside. Look out for the sinuous plant motifs, the playful tower and the stripes of grey and pale stone.

6 The Master's Home

There were plans to turn the step-gabled **Brueghel House** where Pieter Brueghel the Elder lived and died (in 1569) into a museum, but plans were stopped by Belgium's byzantine administrative system. While you can't get inside, you can at least admire the exterior of this venerable building.

7 Local House of Worship

The area's church, **Église Saints-Jeanet-Étienne-aux-Minimes** (Rue des Minimes 62), is a huge, sooty and weather-beaten baroque structure, completed in 1715. If you visit on Sunday at 11.30am, you can go to Mass – the acoustics of the ribbed cupola are very good, and the Mass features either Gregorian chants or Bach cantatas.

8 Time for Fries

Time to relax and grab a bite at the newly reopened **Friture de la Chapelle** for a delicious cone of golden *frites* (fries).

EXPERIENCES

Take in the View on Coudenberg Hill

GARDENS

Connecting the lower town to the Royal Quarter, **Mont des Arts** (MAP: ① P108 **E2**) is built on the slope of the Coudenberg hill, where the palace of the Dukes of Brabant once stood. This urban complex blends culture and calm in the heart of the city.

The formal gardens, originally created for the 1910 World Fair, were redesigned in the 1950s by landscape architect René Pechère in time for Expo '58. They're flanked by the **Bibliothèque Royale** (MAP: ② P108 **E2**) on the right and Square conference centre on the left, as an equestrian statue of King Albert I, Belgium's WWI 'knight-king', welcomes visitors.

In late spring, the rose bushes bloom, fountains trickle and benches fill with sunseekers. Climb the steps and turn around for one of Brussels' best panoramas – a golden view all the way to the Atomium on a clear day. It's especially lovely at sunset, when the gardens softly light up.

Greet the King at His Palace

PALACE

Further up Place Royale, the view opens onto Place des Palais, where major events like the National Day parade take place. Built in the 19th century, the **Palais Royal de Bruxelles** (MAP: ③ P108 **G3**; pictured right; *monarchie.be*) is not the king's residence but his workplace. King Philip lives in Laeken and, like any Belgian, commutes. If the flag is flying, he's in the country. From 23 July to 28 August, the palace is open to visitors, for free. A chance to admire, among other splendid rooms, the Glass gallery and its ceiling covered in millions of jewel beetle wings by contemporary artist, Jan Fabre.

Take a Breather in a Peaceful Park

PARK

The **Parc de Bruxelles** (MAP: ④ P108 **G2**), once a hunting ground, offers a peaceful escape from the city's buzz. It's filled with statues, ponds, a bandstand and outdoor bars. Among its quirks is a stone marking the spot where Russian tsar Peter

🔵 PLACE POELAERT

In front of the Palais de Justice, the wide Place Poelaert offers one of the best panoramic views over Brussels. From here, you can easily spot landmarks like the green-domed Koekelberg Basilica and the iconic Atomium in the distance. Feeling adventurous? A Ferris wheel operates seasonally, lifting visitors even closer to the sky. Half the fun is simply getting there: the famous glass elevator whisks you between the upper town and the Marolles below – providing a free, and brief but dramatic, vertical ride with a view.

TTSTUDIO/SHUTTERSTOCK

the Great, after a night of excess, famously vomited his wine. Beyond the park, the Palais de la Nation houses the Belgian parliament.

Feel Small Facing the Scales of Justice

SIGHT

Looming over Brussels like a menacing giant, the **Palais de Justice** (MAP: 5 P108 **C5**; 1866–83) is one of the largest judicial buildings in the world. Crowned by a colossal cupola, its eclectic interior is as imposing as its exterior. It was designed to evoke the temples of Egypt, Greece and Rome – with a touch of Sumerian influence thrown in. Everything about it, especially its location atop the hill overlooking

the working-class Marolles, was intended to inspire awe for the rule of order and fear of the law.

When its architect, Joseph Poelaert, died during construction (possibly from exhaustion), legends spread that he had been struck down by the witchcraft of the Marolles residents who were evicted to make way for the project. The expression *skieven architek* (twisted architect) remains an insult in the old Bruxellois dialect.

The building has been under renovation since 1984, and an entire generation of Bruxellois has never seen it without scaffolding! The entrance and hallway are freely accessible during the week.

119

Shop Like Crazy at Place du Grand Sablon
SHOPPING

Place du Grand Sablon is renowned for one thing: high-end shopping (particularly antiques) and fancy chocolatiers (Marcolini, Neuhaus, Wittamer…), with some nice restaurants and cafes thrown in for good measure. This is where Pierre Marcolini has his flagship store, and his spring-summer window display is always a seasonal highlight. Enjoy the laid-back, 'quiet luxury' vibe of the neighbourhood, and don't hesitate to explore some of the small side streets to fully immerse yourself in what old Brussels used to feel like. One of them even hides the quirky Museum of Eroticism and Mythology. On Saturdays and Sundays, the square comes alive with its famous **Sablon Antiques Market** (MAP: ⑥ P108 **E4**; pictured right; *sablonantiquesmarket.be; from 9am*) – perfect for treasure hunting or simply browsing.

Salute Bruegel's Spirit at Brussels' Oldest Church
CHURCH

Église Notre-Dame de la Chapelle (MAP: ⑦ P108 **C3**), Brussels' oldest surviving church, now curiously incorporates the decapitated tower of the 1134 original as the central section of a bigger, Gothic edifice. Behind the palm-tree pulpit, look to the wall above a carved confessional to find a small memorial to Petro Brevgello – also known as the artist Pieter Bruegel the Elder, who once lived in nearby Marolles. In front of the church, find a statue of him painting an imaginary scene with a monkey perched on his shoulder.

Take a Break at Petit Sablon
PARK

Not far from Grand Sablon, the charming garden of the **Square du Petit Sablon** (MAP: ⑧ P108 **E4**) is ringed by 48 bronze statuettes representing the medieval guilds. At its centre, standing huddled on a fountain plinth like two actors from a Shakespearean drama, are Counts Egmont and Hoorn – popular city leaders beheaded on the Grand-Place in 1568 for defying Spanish rule. Behind them lies the site of Egmont's former residence, now the **Parc d'Egmont** (MAP: ⑨ P108 **E5**) and one of Brussels' best-kept secrets. You can access it via a staircase a little further behind the square. It's a great spot for a picnic, a peaceful stroll or to say

BRUEGHEL MURALS

To celebrate Brueghel the Elder's impact on art, and Brussels, the city and the collective Farm Prod inaugurated Parcours Bruegel (*parcoursstreetart.brussels/ parcours/parcours-bruegel*), a street-art trail in the Marolles, the neighbourhood the painter used to live in. Eleven murals by different artists revisit the master's works.

PETER HORREE/ALAMY

a quick 'Hi!' to Peter Pan's statue. Or you can book a table at La Fabrique en Ville (p123), the park's cosy eatery, perfect for brunch under the trees.

Swim with a View at Bains de Bruxelles SWIMMING POOL

If you walk past the building just off Place du Jeu-de-Balle without looking up for the 'Bains-Baden' sign, you would never suspect that it houses Brussels city centre's only swimming pool: the **Bains de Bruxelles-Piscine du Centre** (MAP: **10** P108 **B5**). Designed by architect Maurice Van Nieuwenhuyse and opened in 1953, the building incorporates elements of both Art Deco and modernism. The Marolles neighbourhood was once a working-class area with often poorly equipped apartments, and one of the building's original purposes was to provide a public bath where residents could clean themselves and freshen up. This function continues today, alongside its operation as a swimming pool. In fact, there are two pools: a learners' swimming pool where thousands of school children have learned to swim over the decades, and the main swimming pool located on the top floor, featuring a skylight and panoramic views of the Marolles. Swimming here is exhilarating!

LISTINGS

Best Places for...

Ⓔ Budget ⒺⒺ Midrange ⒺⒺⒺ Top End

See p108 for map of locations

Eating

Eating on the Cheap

Friture de la Chapelle Ⓔ
🟢**11** C3

The neighbourhood's *frituur* (chip shop) is back after a makeover! Still run by the same family, so you can be sure the *frites* will be top-notch! *11am-10pm Tue-Sat, to 8pm Sun*

Le Perroquet Ⓔ
🟢**12** D4

This Art Nouveau cafe (pictured right) with stained glass, marble tables and timber panelling, serves drinks and light bites (salads, croque-monsieurs, pittas). An atmospheric, affordable stop. *@leperroquetbruxelles; noon-11.30pm Tue-Sat, to 10.30pm Sun & Mon*

Fine Lunches & Dinners

albert ⒺⒺ
🟢**13** E2

Perched on the library's 5th floor, this 1950s-style spot offers farm-fresh fare, weekend brunches, lush terrace greenery and fantastic city views – one of Brussels' best-kept secrets. *albert.brussels; 10am-5pm*

La Bonne Chère ⒺⒺⒺ
🟢**14** C4

Alexandru Sapco crafts creative seasonal menus in a cosy Marolles house (think Malines chicken with morels and white asparagus). The menu includes Moldovan wines, reflecting the chef's origins. *labonnechere.be; noon-1.30pm & 7-8.30pm Thu & Fri, 7-8.30pm Tue, Wed & Sat*

Les Brigittines ⒺⒺ
🟢**15** C3

In a muted *belle époque* setting, Les Brigittines serves hearty French-Belgian classics – veal cheek, pigs' trotters, steak tartare – with expert staff recommending local beers and artisanal wines. *lesbrigittines.com; noon-2.30pm & 7-10.30pm Mon-Fri*

Vegan Feasts

Het Warm Water ⒺⒺ
🟢**16** B5

Endearing and friendly little vegetarian daytime cafe with stencilled teapots and art collages on the walls. The food – veggie lasagne, soup, curry with coconut – is simple but satisfying. *hetwarmwater.be; 11am-4pm Tue-Sun*

The Judgy Vegan ⒺⒺ
🟢**17** B5

In a quiet Marolles street, this relaxed vegan cafe charms with wood furniture, stone walls and murals. Enjoy seitan 'meatballs', potato burger, lavender lemonade and tempting pastries – plus a laid-back weekend brunch. *thejudgyvegan.com; 6-11pm Thu & Fri, 11.30am-11pm Sat & Sun*

Lucifer Lives ⒺⒺ
🟢**18** C4

Fun and friendly vegan cafe where you can sip your coffee and enjoy a plant-based and homemade lunch or sweets surrounded

SIMON REDDY/ALAMY

by vintage horror and B-movie posters. *@lucilerlivescoffee; 9.30am-4.30pm Tue-Fri, 10am-5pm Sat & Sun*

Coffee, Brunches & Sweet Breaks

Bouche

19 F3

Sleek design, velvet-like brews of carefully selected origins or blends, sinful sweets... No wonder it's been listed as one of the best coffee bars in Belgium. *@bouche.coffee; 7.30am-6pm Mon-Thu, 9am-6pm Fri-Sun*

Café Costermans

20 D3

Tucked away in the courtyard of the townhouse of prestigious antiques merchant Costermans, this is as charming as you'd expect it to be. A little oasis of calm and beauty, from morning till night. *@cafecostermans; 9am-6pm Sat, Sun & Tue, 9am-11pm Wed-Fri*

La Fabrique en Ville

21 E5

In Parc d'Egmont's restored orangery, sunlight floods the tables. Weekdays bring healthy lunches

like falafel salad and indulgent carrot cake; weekends offer an even more extensive brunch spread. *lafabriqueresto. be; 9am-5pm Mon-Fri, 10am-5pm Sat & Sun*

Laurent Gerbaud

22 F2

This bright and welcoming cafe is home to one of the friendliest chocolatiers in town: Laurent Gerbaud. Take a break for hot chocolate, pralines or a pastry and stay for his chocolate-making sessions. *chocolatsgerbaud. be; noon-6pm Tue-Thu, to 6.45pm Fri-Sun*

123

Drinking

Pubs, Cafes & Beer

Chaff
 A5

This friendly alternative bistro on Place du Jeu-de-Balle is the perfect spot for a coffee break after browsing the flea market or grabbing a bite. Enjoy concerts and game nights in the evening. *@le_chaff; 5pm-1am Mon, 8.30am-midnight Tue-Sat, 8.30am-4.30pm Sun.*

Chez Richard
24 **D3**

Place du Sablon's most Parisian cafe. Unpretentious and friendly place where locals come by for a glass of wine, a cocktail or something to eat (from shrimp croquettes to seafood platters). Open late. *chezrichard.be; 11.30am-midnight Sun-Thu, 11.30am-1am Fri & Sat*

Le Petit Lion
25 **B5**

The Marolles' last *bruin café* where elderly locals play cards by day and younger patrons gather by afternoon, valuing its authentic spirit amid the neighbourhood's gentrification. *10am-11pm*

Mon-Fri, 9.30am-2am Sat, 9.30am-11pm Sun

Mazette
 A6

A cooperative cafe, microbrewery, bakery and soft drink maker serving scratch-made food from local ingredients. Beer is brewed downstairs and bread baked on-site. *mazette.brussels; 5pm-midnight Mon, 11am-midnight Wed & Thu, 11am-1am Fri, 10am-1am Sat, 10am-6pm Sun*

Nightlife

GIMIC Radio
 B5

In one of the Marolles' most atmospheric streets, GIMIC Radio is a disco-bar and online station showcasing local DJs set in a raw, quirky old house with an inner terrace. A great place to start the night. *gimicradio.com; 2pm-late Wed-Sun*

Fuse
 A6

The Marolles club (pictured right) that 'invented' European techno still crams up to 2000 people onto its two dance floors. Once a month, it hosts La Démence, a legendary gay rave drawing men from across Europe and beyond. *fuse.be; 11pm-7am*

Cocktail Time

Vertigo
 D3

Hidden in Brussels' oldest inn, this cocktail bar/restaurant is full of surprises: a wood-filled, armchair-strewn interior, a charming courtyard, inventive drinks and a globe-trotting menu. Plus brunch on Sundays. *vertigobrussels.com; 6pm-midnight Wed-Fri, 3pm-midnight Sat, noon-8pm Sun*

Öken
30 **D5**

Don't be fooled by its private-club address: Öken, the Merode's 70-seat underground bar, welcomes all to its minimalist, zen-like space for lab-inspired cocktails and late-night dancing. *oken.be; 7pm-1am Thu & Sat, to 3am Fri*

Shopping

Green & Ethical Shopping

Jinzu
31 **B5**

A gem amid the Marolles' many shops, showcasing ethical, mostly European creators, from recycled Spanish textiles to

SINCE 1994

Belgian ceramics hand-picked, or made, by owner Eloïse Bonehill. *jinzu.be; 11am-6pm Mon & Thu-Sat, noon-5pm Sun*

Vintage Galore
Bernard Gavilan Since 1994
32 B5

No less than three stores are dedicated to vintage pieces from 1900 to 1990, all located in the Marolles, the neighbourhood where Bernard Gavilan, the king of vintage, grew up. Your finds can even be altered on demand. *10am-6pm*

Foxhole Vintage
33 B5

Vintage and used clothing are given a hip twist at this iconic address, plus heaps of accessories – especially leather, hats and sunglasses. Most pieces, from the 1950s to 1990s, hail from Europe or the USA. *foxholevintage. com; 10am-6pm Thu-Sun*

Antiques
Passage 125
34 B5

One of the largest antique stores in Brussels: 1200m2 of vintage furniture, religious trinkets, 19th-century paintings, sculptures from Africa and Asia – even a piece of a mammoth's jaw! But it's especially famous for selling stained glass. *passage125.com; 10am-5.30pm Tue-Fri & Sun, 10am-6pm Sat*

Via Antica
35 C4

Even though Via Antica carries 18th-century furniture, the store focuses more on the 20th, particularly mid-century and 1970s pieces. If you're looking for an Italian Murano glass chandelier or a Scandinavian design cabinet, you're in the right place. *viaantica. be; 10am-6pm*

See p139 for eating, drinking and shopping listings

Explore
EU Quarter & Etterbeek

Researched by
Mélissa Monaco

The EU Quarter and Etterbeek has a reputation for thundering traffic and office blocks, and is, of course, the heart of European politics – whether that's an enticement or a deterrent is up to you – but there is plenty here to attract visitors. The area around Parc du Cinquantenaireis Brussels' second-largest museum hub after the Royal Quarter, with collections dedicated to art and history, the military and automobiles. If you're into architecture, strolling around the ponds of Square Marie-Louise, Ave Palmerston and Square Ambiorix is pure pleasure. The streets are lined with fine houses and two Art Nouveau masterpieces: the Hôtel Van Eetvelde and the Maison Saint-Cyr.

Getting Around

 Metro

The closest stop for the museums Is Mérode; to explore the EU sights, head to Schuman. For Square Marie-Louise, get off at Maelbeek.

 Bus

Bus 95 from the city centre stops at Place du Luxembourg, in front of the EU Parliament.

 **On foot**

The EU Parliament is a pleasant half-hour walk from Grand-Place and the city hall; you can cross the leafy Parc du Bruxelles en route.

THE BEST

EUROPEAN PAST & PRESENT
House of European History (p133)

POLITICAL INSIGHTS
EU Parliament (p132)

HISTORY & ART
Musée Art & Histoire (p130)

GREEN LUNGS
Parc du Cinquantenaire (p136)

FAMOUS FRITES
Maison Antoine (p139)

Parc du Cinquantenaire (p136)
WERNER LEROOY/SHUTTERSTOCK

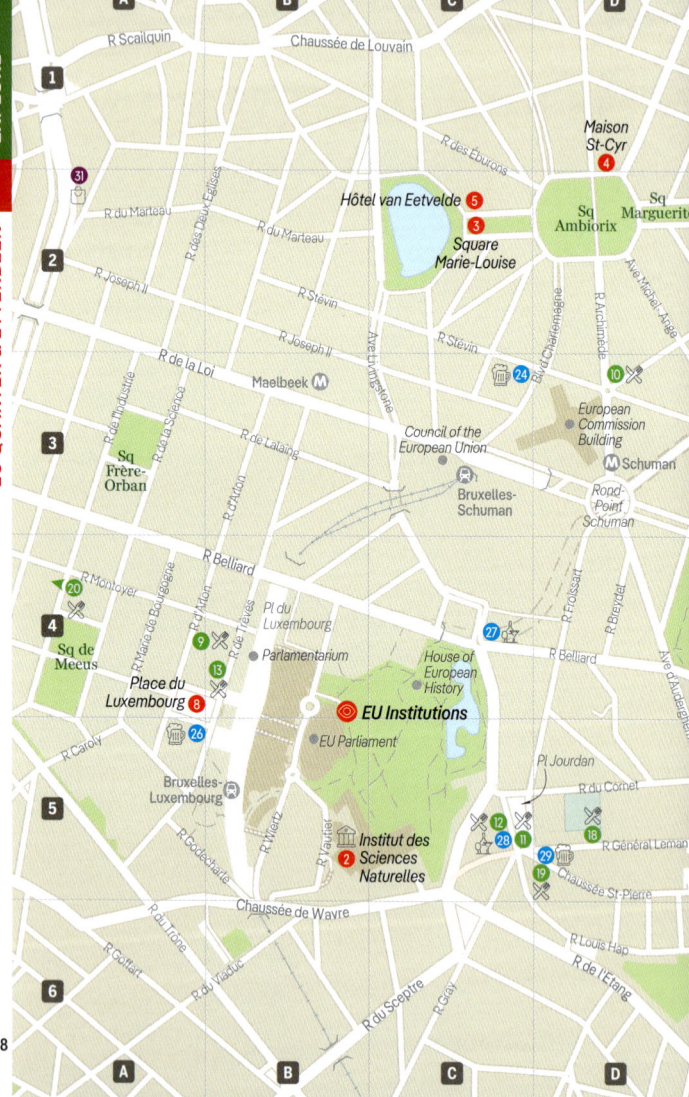

A **B** **C** **D**

1

R Scailquin

Chaussée de Louvain

R des Eburons

Maison
St-Cyr
4

31

R du Marteau

Hôtel van Eetvelde **5**

3

Sq
Ambiorix

Sq
Marguerite

R des Deux Églises

R du Marteau

2

R Joseph II

R des Deux Églises

R Stevin

Square
Marie-Louise

Ave Michel-Ange

R Joseph II

R Stevin

Ave d'Auderghem

R de la Loi

Maelbeek **M**

24

10

Sq
Frère-
Orban

R de l'Industrie

R de la Science

R de Laláine

R d'Arlon

Council of the
European Union

European
Commission
Building

M Schuman

3

Bruxelles-
Schuman

Rond-
Point
Schuman

R Belliard

R Montoyer

20

Pl du
Luxembourg

27

R Belliard

R Froissart

R Breydel

4

Sq de
Meeus

R Marie de Bourgogne

R d'Arlon

R de Trèves

9

Parlamentarium

House of
European
History

13

Place du
Luxembourg **8**

26

◎ *EU Institutions*

• EU Parliament

Pl Jourdan

R du Cornet

Bruxelles-
Luxembourg

12

18

R Général Leman

R Caroly

R Wiertz

R Vautier

28 **11**

29

19

R de l'Étang

5

R Godecharle

Institut des
2 Sciences
Naturelles

Chaussée St-Pierre

Chaussée de Wavre

R du Trône

R Gaffart

R du Viaduc

R Louis Hap

6

R du Sceptre

R Gray

A **B** **C** **D**

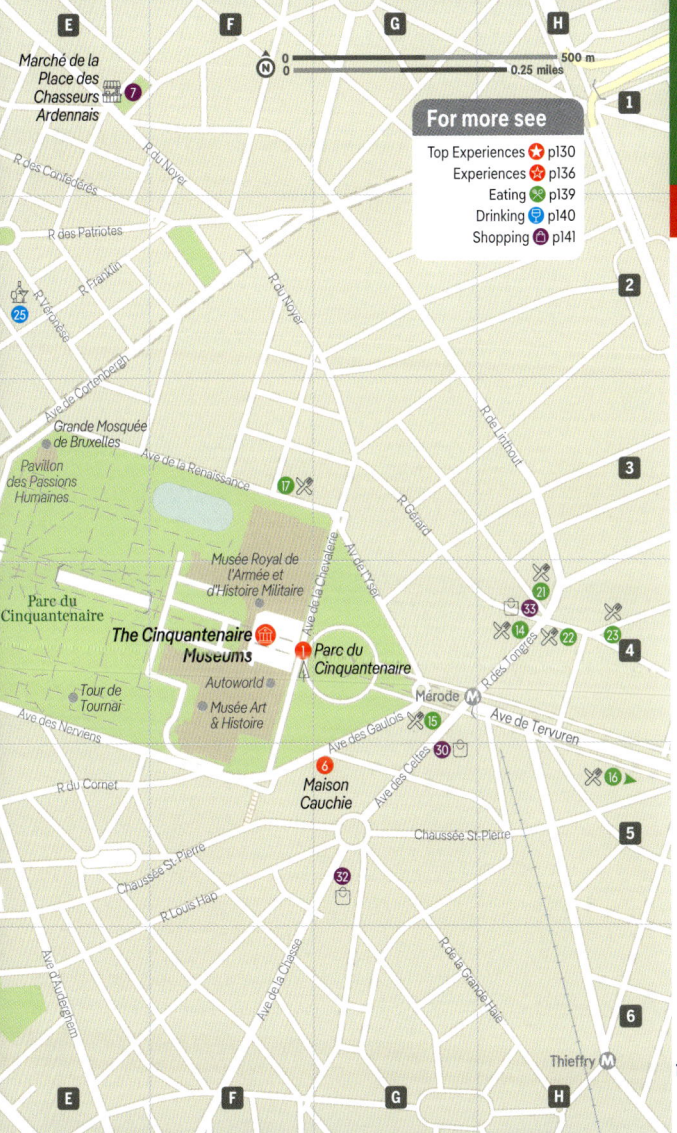

E   F   G   H

EXPLORE

EU QUARTER & ETTERBEEK

Marché de la
Place des
Chasseurs
Ardennais   7

N 0   500 m
   0   0.25 miles

1

For more see

Top Experiences ⭐ p130
Experiences ⭐ p136
Eating 🍴 p139
Drinking 🍷 p140
Shopping 🛍 p141

2

R des Confédérés

R du Noyer

R des Patriotes

R Franklin

25

Ave de Cortenbergh

R de Linthout

Grande Mosquée
de Bruxelles

Pavillon
des Passions
Humaines

Ave de la Renaissance

17

R Gérard

3

R du Noyer

Ave de l'Yser

Ave de la Chevalerie

Musée Royal de
l'Armée et
d'Histoire Militaire

21

33

14

22

23

4

Parc du
Cinquantenaire

**The Cinquantenaire
Museums**   1 Parc du
              Cinquantenaire

R des Tongres

Autoworld

Mérode Ⓜ

Tour de
Tournai

Musée Art
& Histoire

15

Ave de Tervuren

16

Ave des Nerviens

Ave des Gaulois

30

R du Cornet

6

Maison
Cauchie

Ave des Celtes

5

Chaussée St-Pierre

Chaussée St-Pierre

32

R Louis Hap

R de la Grande Haie

Ave de la Chasse

6

Ave d'Auderghem

Thieffry Ⓜ

129

★ TOP EXPERIENCE

The Cinquantenaire Museums

Built in 1880 for Belgium's 50th anniversary, Parc du Cinquantenaire (p136) is famed for its triple-arched monument and arcades, leafy lanes and many public art works. Around it, three museums await offering unique journeys through art history, automobiles and military heritage.

MAP P128 **F4**

PLANNING TIP
Only have one day? Pick one or two museums to visit, as their collections are particularly extensive: Musée Art & Histoire can take a whole day alone.

Scan this QR code for opening hours and tickets.

Musée Art & Histoire

This astonishingly rich collection ranges from ancient Egyptian sarcophagi and Meso-American masks to icons and wooden bicycles. New rooms, opened in 2025, display decorative art from the 19th and 20th centuries. Decide what you want to see before your visit or the sheer scope may overwhelm. Visually attractive spaces include Victor Horta's reconstructed winter garden, which he designed for engineer Jean Cousin, and the soaring Corinthian columns (convincing fibreglass props) that bring atmosphere to an original mosaic from Roman Syria. Labelling is mainly in French and Dutch, so consider the English-language audio guide (€3).

Musée Royal de l'Armée et d'Histoire Militaire

See extensive displays of weaponry, uniforms, vehicles, warships, paintings, documentation, even planes, all dating from the medieval period through to Belgian independence and the World Wars. You can climb to the top of the arch (or take the lift) for sweeping city views. Among the curiosities is the aviation hall, with around 100 aircraft and flying objects like air balloons, some of them suspended from the gallery's glass roof, and an astonishing collection of tsarist Russia militaria. The museum is going through renovation at the time of writing so don't be surprised if some parts aren't accessible.

CRISTIAN PUSCASU/SHUTTERSTOCK

Autoworld

Until very recently, Belgium was known for its car factories (there's only one remaining today), so no wonder it's got a museum dedicated to four-wheelers. Autoworld (pictured above; *autoworld.be*) displays one of Europe's biggest ensembles of vintage and 20th-century vehicles, based on the passion of avid car collector Ghislain Mahy. Among the gleaming exhibits, you'll notice a Harley-Davidson, a present from the police force to former King Albert II. He gifted it to the museum when he decided his biker days were over. Zones inside the museum include the Cars of Tintin, defunct Belgian cars, royal vehicles and the history of electric cars. Also check for temporary exhibitions that might pique your interest.

QUICK BREAK
You can refuel at a cafe-restaurant at the Musée Art & Histoire. For a more extensive choice, Le Pré aux Clercs (p140) nearby specialises in grilled meats.

★ TOP EXPERIENCE

EU Institutions

Most European Union bodies are located in Brussels, marking the urban landscape with their presence and giving it a distinctly cosmopolitan character. If you want to understand how these institutions work, impacting the lives of over 450 million Europeans, a visit offers valuable insights.

MAP P128 **B4**

PLANNING TIP
If you are short on time, prioritise the Parlamentarium or the House of European History, depending on your interest. Always have your ID with you when visiting.

Scan this QR code for opening hours and tickets.

EU Parliament & Parlamentarium

As the only directly elected EU body, the EU Parliament is closest to the people – and visits are free but must be booked in advance. An audio guide in 24 languages is provided, or you can use the 'EP Visit' app. Want to dive deeper? Book the Hemicycle talk with a guide to better understand how it all works. For the ultimate experience, visit during a plenary session to see MEPs in action. Seats for the debates are limited, so be sure to register in advance.

Right across from the Parliament, the Parlamentarium brings the EU to life with fun, interactive exhibits. Step into a 360° panorama of the Parliament, explore the map of all member states, or listen to personal stories about how EU laws impact daily life.

EU Commission & Council

The star-shaped Berlaymont Building, home to the European Commission, has become an EU icon in Brussels. Built in 1967 on the former site of a convent, it houses the offices of the President and Commissioners. Look closely and you'll see that only its central core touches the ground, while four branches appear to float like tree limbs. It's closed to the public but the nearby **Experience Europe** exhibition centre is open to all.

©VISIT.BRUSSELS - JEAN-PAUL REMY

At the **Council of the European Union**, visitors can explore the welcome centre and admire the striking 'egg' structure encased within the building.

House of European History

Housed in Parc Léopold's beautifully renovated Eastman Building, the airy and elegant House of European History (pictured above; *brusselsmuseums. be*) takes you into some dark corners of European history, from war and destruction to the biggest peace project ever endeavoured. The new 6th-floor 'Europe Now' exhibition is dedicated to challenges and opportunities facing Europe today (immigration, terrorism, climate change…) but also what brings Europeans together. The highly (overly?) interactive experience takes about 1.5 hours. Roam through permanent and temporary exhibitions in any of 24 languages.

TAKE A BREAK
After visiting the Parlamentarium and/or Parliament, Place du Luxembourg is lined with cafes but you can also take a 10-minute trek to Maison Antoine (p139) for their famous *frites* (fries).

WALKING TOUR

Walk Art Nouveau Brussels

Art Nouveau is the signature architectural style of Brussels. Its most significant exponent was Victor Horta (1861–1947), mostly remembered for his daring, light-suffused buildings constructed with wrought iron and glass. Some of his surviving masterpieces, and plenty by his contemporaries, can be explored on this route.

START	END	LENGTH
Porte de Hal	Hôtel Solvay	3.5km; 2hr

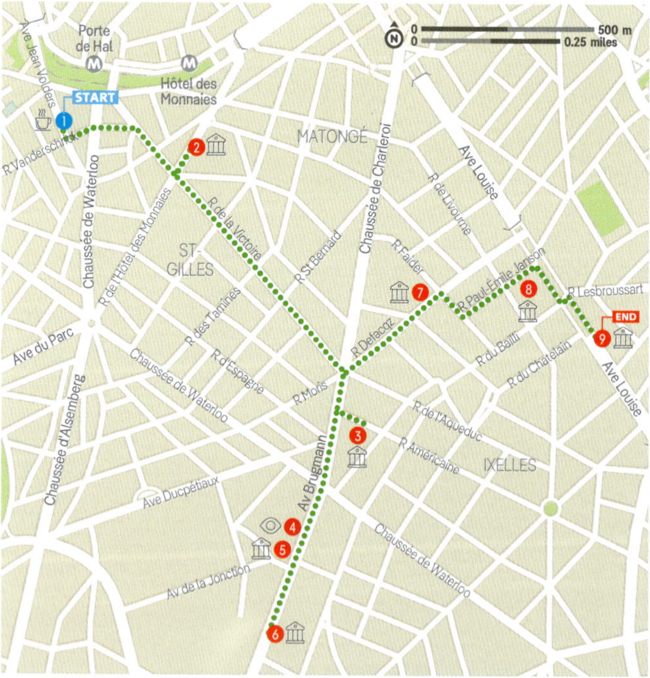

1 Watering Hole

Take Chaussée de Waterloo from Porte de Hal, then turn right onto Ave Jean Volders. At No 48, visit the classic Art Nouveau **La Porteuse d'Eau** for coffee, known for its stunning stained-glass ceiling and ornate wooden booths.

2 A Sober Horta

The **Hôtel Winssinger**, at Rue de l'Hôtel des Monnaies 66, is a typically sober, un-ostentatious Horta building. Look for the characteristic pale stone, the use of metal around the windows and the dainty swirling balconies.

3 The Master's House & Workshop

You may want to visit **Musée Horta** separately to give yourself enough time to see everything. But if this isn't possible, do stop to admire the exterior – characteristically simple, but featuring a playful motif on the dragonfly terrace. You'll find it at Rue Américaine 27.

4 Two Owls

Av Brugmann reveals two charming adjacent buildings: Maison Hannon, and Édouard Pelseneer's **Les Hiboux** (No 55), adorned with Gothic owls and graffiti. Pelseneer's father, Henri, was a furniture-maker who worked for Horta.

5 Swirling Stairwell

Jules Brunfaut's **Maison Hannon** is open to the public. Make time to book a visit, as the renovated interior features a stunning greenhouse, and the swirling fresco adorning the stairwell magically whisks you away to the upper floor.

6 House of Cuba

Ave Brugmann 80 is **Maison-atelier Fernand Dubois**. It's another Horta building, commissioned by Horta's designer friend, Fernand Dubois, who worked with him on Hôtel Tassel, and it's now the Cuban embassy. Notice the strong asymmetry between the left (the living quarters) and the right (Dubois' workshop).

7 Extravagant Abode

Architect Paul Hankar's buildings on Rue Defacqz are much more exuberant than Horta's. At Rue Defacqz 71, **Maison Hankar** was designed by Hankar and used as his studio. Take time to admire the graffiti.

8 Art Nouveau's Manifesto

Rue Paul-Émile Janson 6 is the site of Horta's first truly Art Nouveau house, the 1893 **Hôtel Tassel**. Horta designed the mosaics, stained glass, woodwork...even the door handles.

9 Cherry on the Cake

At No 224 Ave Louise, you'll find the Horta-designed **Hôtel Solvay**, considered one of his masterpieces and no wonder! Armand Solvay was a member of one of the richest families in Belgium, an industrial dynasty whose company still exists today. The mansion is open to the public, and tours last 40 minutes.

EXPERIENCES

Chill at Parc du Cinquantenaire   PARK

After visiting the museums, take time to admire the Cinquantenaire arcades before relaxing in the vast **park** (MAP: ❶ P128 **F4**) at their feet. Built in 1880 to mark Belgium's 50th anniversary, the arcades were redesigned in 1905 by architect Gédéon Bordiau as a four-column triumphal arch. Each column bears bronze allegories of eight Belgian provinces, while Brabant crowns the monument, driving a quadriga and raising the national flag.

The surrounding park, laid out in strict French-style geometry, offers a peaceful pause amid statues, fountains and curiosities. Look out for the Tour de Tournai, a small medieval tower that seems straight from a children's fairy tale. In the summer, a shaded open-air bar offers a welcome respite from the sun. The park also houses Belgium's largest mosque, near the Pavillon des Passions Humaines.

Get Close to Dinosaurs at the Institut des Sciences Naturelles   MUSEUM

A kids' favourite, the **Institut des Sciences Naturelles** (MAP: ❷ P128 **B5**; *naturalsciences.be; adult/concession €10/5*) is not only a natural science museum, it's also a highly recognised research centre. Of course, the highlight of the visit is the impressive collection of 28 iguanodons found in a Belgian coal mine. The gallery displaying these dinosaurs (and others such as the gigantic Diplodocus or terrifying T-Rex) is the largest of its kind in Europe. Highly interactive and entertaining, it's really difficult not to spend at least two hours here. Do not miss the Evolution Gallery, Man Gallery or the Mineral Room. The Living Planet exhibit (inside the Evolution Gallery) and BiodiverCITY (about urban fauna and flora in Brussels) will keep you amazed at how resilient our natural world is. The museum also hosts temporary exhibitions.

 SCANDALOUS MARBLE

On 1 October 1899, Jef Lambeaux' colossal marble relief *Les Passions Humaines* was unveiled inside a neoclassical pavilion by Victor Horta. Stretching 12m, it portrayed humanity's condition and struggles, maternity, seduction, lust, rape, suicide, war, all presided over by Death. Its writhing mass of nude bodies scandalised contemporaries, and the notion of Death supreme even over the figure of Jesus outraged Catholics. Days later, the entrance to the pavilion was boarded up. Forgotten, it survived both World Wars unscathed. Today, the pavilion opens only occasionally, heightening the aura of mystery around one of Belgium's most provocative masterpieces.

©VISIT.BRUSSELS · JEAN-PAUL REMY

Peek at 19th-Century Brussels

GREEN SPACE

At **Square Marie-Louise** (MAP: ❸ P128 **C2**), you can feed the ducks in the pretty tree-lined pond that's surrounded by greenery and a smattering of Art Nouveau architecture. Sit down on a bench, enjoy the water shoots when the weather is fine and push towards nearby Parc Ambiorix (further down the pond) to admire an Art Nouveau jewel: the narrow **Maison Saint-Cyr** (MAP: ❹ P128 **D1**). The building has a classic 1903 facade that's remarkable for its naturalistic copper-framed window, filigree balconies and circular upper portal. It's crowned by a devil-may-care topknot of extravagantly twisted ironwork.

Feel Out of Africa at Hôtel van Eetvelde

ARCHITECTURE

Hôtel van Eetvelde (MAP: ❺ P128 **C2**; pictured above; *lab-an.be; €10*), which houses the Art Nouveau Laboratory, is now open to the public. While the outside of this building is not the city's most gripping, its interior is a Horta masterpiece. It's studded with exotic timbers and sports a central glass dome infused with African-inspired plant motifs. Its owner, Baron Van Eetvelde, was at that time (1895) Minister for the Congo and, not coincidentally, the country's highest-paid civil servant.

Gawk at Maison Cauchie's Gracious Sgraffito   ARCHITECTURE

Built in 1905, stunning **Maison Cauchie** (MAP: **6** P128 **G5**; *cauchie. be; adult/child €9.50/free*) was the home of architect and painter Paul Cauchie (1875–1952), and his wife, Caroline Voet, also an artist. Its sgraffito facade, adorned with graceful female figures, is one of the most beautiful in Brussels. It looks like a Klimt painting transformed into architecture. A petition saved the house from demolition in 1971, and since 1975 it has been a protected monument and can be visited at the weekends.

Mingle at Marché de la Place des Chasseurs Ardennais   MARKET

What began as a small neighbourhood **market** (MAP: **7** P128 **E1**; *1030 .be/fr/lieu-commerce/marche-place -des-chasseurs-ardennais; 2-8pm Fri*) has grown into a buzzing weekly rendezvous. Alongside the producers' stalls, many offering organic food and fresh produce, visitors gather to socialise at the numerous food and drink stands for an after-work aperitif. The market's timing and its proximity to the European Commission make it a favourite among the EU crowd.

EU Bubble at Place du Luxembourg   AFTER-WORK VIBES

Place du Luxembourg (MAP: **8** P128 **A4**), Place Lux or PLux as it's often called, suddenly comes alive on Thursdays. Bars are chock-full of patrons, if the weather permits, terraces are completely filled and the air buzzes with excitement and the sound of dozens of languages. It's the quintessential *apéro* spot for Eurocrats, interns, expats and lobbyists who spill out of the European Parliament after work to mingle over beers, wine and cocktails. The atmosphere is festive and slightly chaotic, with suited professionals rubbing shoulders with students and locals. If you're after Brussels' most international after-work scene, this is the place.

 THE GOD'S WHIM

Brussels' EU Parliament goes by an unflattering nickname: Caprice des Dieux (the God's Whim). Locals couldn't help noticing that the building's gleaming oval facade looks strikingly like the famous French soft cheese of the same name, sold in its iconic oval box. And a fitting nickname it was, as the building cost a fortune; swathes of the Léopold neighbourhood had to be destroyed, its inhabitants slowly forced to leave to make way for this lofty project. And so the comparison quickly stuck, a perfect example of Belgian wit deflating the pomp of European politics.

Best Places for...

€ Budget **€€** Midrange **€€€** Top End

See p128 for map of locations

Eating

On the Cheap

Caffè Italiano €
9 A4

A slice of Italy if you're craving a real espresso or *tramezzino* (sandwich). Careful: it's packed at lunchtime! The second location at Schuman is open a bit later and on Saturday. @caffeitaliano. bruxelles; 8am-4pm Mon-Fri

Le Botaniste €
10 D3

Vegetarians and vegans, rejoice! This stylish canteen has you covered with satisfying bowls of vegan-twisted comfort food (pasta Bolognese or chilli sin carne), and desserts. *lebotaniste .eu/en; 8.30am-9.30pm Mon-Fri, 11.30am-9.30pm Sat & Sun*

Maison Antoine €
11 C5

A Brussels institution where locals, expats and even dignitaries queue for a cone of twice-fried beef-fat chips. Though some say quality has slipped, it remains iconic. *maisonantoine.be; 11.30am-1am*

Casual & Affordable

Brasserie Signature €€
12 C5

A decades-old fixture on busy Place Jourdan, this brasserie serves up Belgian classics *(moules-frites, steak-frites...)* along with lobsters you can pick straight from the tank. Nab a terrace seat if you can. *brasseriesignature. be; noon-11pm*

Domenica €€
13 B4

Selling honest, ethically sourced lunches to a predominantly Eurocrat crowd, Domenica holds up its values of quality and sustainability with home-made pasta, lush ciabattas and, of course, delicious coffee. *domenica.eu.com; 8am-3pm*

LATYPIQ €€
14 H4

This playful spot takes the humble taco globetrotting: smash-burger bites for the USA, tofu for Japan, *vitello tonnato* for Italy. Still peckish? Sweet and savoury pancakes to finish will fill you up. Fun, fast and tasty. *latypiq.be; 9am-10pm Mon-Sat, to 5pm Sun*

La Terrasse €€
15 G4

Close to the Cinquante-naire, this wood-panelled classic cafe has a tree-shaded terrace and makes an ideal refreshment stop after a hard day's 'museuming'. Snacks, sweet treats, brasserie dishes and decent mussels are available at various times. *brasserielaterrasse.be; 10am-midnight Sun-Wed, to 1am Thu-Sat*

Fine Lunch & Dinner

Le Monde Est Petit €€€
16 H5

In the elegant Square Montgomery district, Loïc Villers runs this chic, velvet-adorned, yet cosy spot. The short, seasonal menu is market-driven and creative, with pitch-perfect sauces and warm, attentive service. *lemondeestpetit.be; noon-2pm & 7-9.30pm Tue-Fri*

Le Pré aux Clercs €€

17 F3

This discreet restaurant just by the Cinquante-naire will win you over if you like meat (the speciality): delectable grilled matured beef, duck, fish...in a plush setting. *lepreauxclercs.be; 11am-11pm Tue-Sat, noon-5pm Sun*

Origine €€

18 D5

Under the motto 'love, drink and eat', Origine offers seasonal dishes beneath a Hello Monster fresco. The several-course menu lets you mix cold, warm, hot and sweet options like chimichurri squid or veal with cardamom-lemon purée. *origine-restaurant.be/en; 7-9.30pm Mon-Thu, noon-2pm & 7-9.30pm Fri*

Stirwen €€€

19 D5

This long-standing Franco-Belgian spot draws a discerning EU crowd. Recently refreshed decor and young chef François-Xavier Lambory inject new energy into its otherwise classic menu.

stirwen.be; 7-9.30pm Tue, noon-2.30pm & 7-9.30pm Wed-Fri, 7am-9.30pm Sat

Coffee & Sweet Spots

Caffelatte Espressobar

20 A4

Fancy Italian coffee bar serving classic *cappuccini* and *cornetti alla crema*, plus indulgent flavoured *espressini* (the tiramisu one is to die for), pistachio-filled croissants, pastries and *focaccie*. *caffelatte.be; 7.30am-5.30pm Mon-Fri*

Nicolas Koulepis

21 H4

From Rhodes to Brussels, top pastry chef Nicolas Koulepis blends French classics with Greek specialities. Don't miss his addictive *ekmek tsoureki*: brioche with spiced syrup, walnuts, almonds and whipped cream. *nikolas koulepis.com; 8am-7pm Tue-Sat, to 2pm Sun*

Petit Bé

22 H4

If you're watching your carbs but have a sweet tooth, this artisan bakery specialises in low-glycemic index pastries. All items are labelled with their index, so you can indulge with confidence. *petitbe.be; 10am-6pm Tue-Sun*

Tulipe

23 H4

Tucked into a corner house near the Parc du Cinquantenaire, this cosy coffee bar charms with exposed brick, jazz tunes, yummy coffee, pastries and sunny terrace. *tulipe. coffee; 8am-6pm Mon-Fri, 9.30am-6pm Sat & Sun*

Drinking

After Work

Kitty O'Shea's

24 C3

Friendly Irish pub near the European Commission that's great for beer, sport, socialising and sat-isfying a sudden craving for fish and chips or beef and Guinness pie. Plus live gigs. *kittyosheas.be; noon-1am*

Piola Libri

25 E2

Italophiles relax after work on sofas, at pavement tables or in the tiny triangle of the back garden and enjoy *aperitivo* with chilled white wines at this con-vivial bookshop-bar-cafe. It also has an eclectic programme of readings and DJ nights. *piolalibri.be; noon-10pm Mon-Sat*

Ginette Bar
 A5

One of the best drinking-and-eating holes on Plux, linked to the Ginette brewery. The shaded terrace is perfect in fine weather, and when it rains a large skylight helps fill the funky interior with as much light as possible. *ginettebars.com; 11am-2am Mon-Sat*

Grand Central
 C4

Grand Central sprawls across two floors, drawing crowds with a menu suiting every moment: light lunches; boards to share with an aperitif; and hearty burgers and bar food by night. The happy hour is a bargain. *legrandcentral.com; noon-midnight Mon-Thu, noon-1am Fri, 11am-1am Sat, 11am-10.30pm Sun*

Good for Beers

L'Espérance (chez Bernard)
 C5

Traditional *bruin café* that seems to have been here on Place Jourdan since forever. The beer menu is as classic as its wood-panelled decor (Belgian ales and Trappist). Best perk: you can bring your fries from Maison Antoine if you buy a drink. *7.30am-late*

Beers Bank
 D5

Place Jourdan's liveliest bar. Patrons happily break their vaults (and kegs) daily: there are nearly 200 beers to raid! Can't decide? The cheerful, knowledgeable staff will happily steer you in the right direction. *beersbank. be; 3.30pm-1am Mon-Thu, 3.30pm-2.30am Fri & Sat, noon-midnight Sun*

Shopping

Something Tasty to Bring Back

HOP!
 G5

It's a wine and beer cellar, a fine groceries shop and a gourmet caterer all wrapped into one small store that is chock-full of bottles, boxes, cans and jars with everything you need to make a perfect aperitif. *hop.brussels; 10.30am-8pm Mon-Sat*

L'Heure Bleue
 A2

'The blue hour', that fleeting moment before night, gives its name to Muriel and Olivier's shop: she crafts and curates jewellery, while he shares his passion for fine teas, especially *pu-erh* and Liu Bao. *lheurebleue. net; noon-6pm Tue-Fri, to 4pm Sat*

Pralins
 G5

There's a new female chocolatier in town. Vivian Lins, trained by master chocolatier and pastry chef Yasushi Sasaki, has just struck out on her own, bringing exotic flavours from her native Brazil into creations like her açai-beer praline. *@pra.lins; 10.30am-6.30pm Tue-Sat*

Precious Gifts

Lucie in the R
II4

Looking for gifts with a purpose? This concept store offers cosmetics, accessories and home decor curated by Emilie and Laurence according to their values: all recycled, upcycled, locally made or crafted from natural and organic materials. *lucieinther. com; 10am-6.30pm Tue-Sat*

Bruges & Brussels Toolkit

Markt (p38)
ECSTK22 / SHUTTERSTOCK

Family Travel

Brussels and Bruges are great for families. Fairy-tale-like Bruges will enchant the children while Brussels has tons of activities and museums for kids of all ages.

Child Friendly?

Brussels and Bruges are great family destinations. In Brussels, children are going to love the comics museum or the natural sciences museum with its dinosaurs. Bruges, meanwhile, feels like a storybook come alive, with swan-filled canals, boat rides and chocolate at every corner: pure magic for kids and parents alike.

Eating Out with Children

You won't have to stick to fast food, as many restaurants (especially casual ones) offer children's menus and are well prepared to accommodate their youngest customers with highchairs and diaper-changing facilities in the restrooms. In Brussels, food courts such as **Wolf** (p103) have become increasingly popular and serve as a fantastic option for families.

Cooling Off

Brussels' Place de Brouckère and Place de la Bourse have fountains where children can play in summer.

Public Transport

Travelling with a pram? Most Brussels metro stations have elevators. Trams and buses (including those in Bruges) provide space for prams. Children under six can ride for free.

FAMILY-FRIENDLY BRUSSELS

Visit Brussels has compiled an extensive selection of museums and activities suited for the whole family. Scan the QR code.

Free Museums

Musea Brugge (*museabrugge.be*) sites are free for kids under 13 (except the Belfort). In Brussels, many museums are free for people under 18.

Accommodation

Staying in Brussels and Bruges is expensive, even in hostels, but you'll save by visiting off-season or on a Sunday.

Where to Stay if You Love...

Being in the Centre of It All

Grand-Place (p81) Brussels' hub with sights, bars, restaurants, shopping and Central Station within 10 minutes' walk. Convenient, but expect some noise.

Art, Parks & Fanciness

Royal Quarter (p107) A quiet and upscale part of Brussels. Plenty of museums, elegant stores, fine-dining restaurants and proximity to several parks.

OUR PICK

We Love to Stay in...

Sint-Anna (p46). To the east of the Bruges city centre, 18th-century windmills and little whitewashed cottages lend the Sint-Anna district a distinctly village-like air. This quiet residential area is great if you want to get away from it all and hole up in a flower-wreathed little corner of paradise, Bruges-style.

HOW MUCH FOR A NIGHT IN

Hostel dorm bed
€35

Midrange hotel
€130

Luxury hotel **€300**

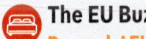

The EU Buzz

Brussels' EU Quarter (p127) Not the liveliest part of town, except for Place Lux, but it has solid accommodation options with prices slashed during the weekend.

Dreamy Canal View

Bruges' centre (p35) You'll find budget-friendly B&Bs or palatial stays. By night, gaze at canals shimmering in the moonlight – a magical, romantic cityscape.

Tranquillity

South Bruges (p57) Away from the tourist hotspots, Bruges takes on a more residential air and the streets are sleepy come nightfall. Stay in a gabled building.

145

 Food, Drink & Nightlife

Allergies & Intolerances

Most restaurants and cafes have allergens listed on their menu. If in doubt ask the waitstaff.

HOW TO SAY

I'm allergic to... *Je suis allergique à (singular)/aux (plural)... / Ik ben allergisch voor...*

...nuts *fruits à coques / schaalvruchten (noten)*

...seafood *fruits de mer / zeevruchten*

...dairy products *produits laitiers / melkprodukten*

...gluten *gluten*

Does this contain nuts? *Est-ce que ça contient des fruits à coque? / Bevat dit schaalvruchten (noten)?*

?
HOW TO ASK...
Is there a vegan option?
Y a t-il une option végane? / Is er een veganistische optie?
Is this gluten free?
Est-ce sans gluten? / Is dit glutenvrij?

— EAT MUSSELS —

The Belgian national dish deserves respect so here's how to enjoy it properly. Use your first empty shell as pincers for *frites* (chips) and mussels. Discard shells in the upturned saucepan lid and avoid closed ones, as they're uncooked. Finish with the flavour-packed broth. A finger rinse is usually provided.

Frites Sauces

Eating *frites/frietjes* without a sauce is akin to a crime in Belgium.

Mayonnaise: The egg and mustard–based classic.

Andalouse: Tomato, sweet chilli and mustard.

Samouraï: Spicy red-pepper sauce.

Américaine: Spicy-sweet tomato sauce with onions and peppers.

Brasil: Sweet-and-sour sauce with tomato and pineapple.

HOW TO... Pay the Bill

Paying the bill is straightforward: taxes and service charges are included. At restaurants, you'll need to ask for it.

Tipping isn't necessary unless you want to reward exceptional service.

The bill, please *L'addition, s'il vous plaît / De rekening, alstublieft*

Splitting the bill is usually possible, though some places may not allow it, especially if you mix cash and card payments. It's best to ask first.

Can we split the bill? *Pouvons-nous diviser l'addition? / Kunnen we de rekening splitsen?*

In cash or by card? *En liquide ou par carte? / Cash of met kaart?*

PRICE RANGES

The following price ranges refer to the average cost of a main course.

€ less than €18
€€ €19–28
€€€ above €28

OPENING HOURS

Cafes/coffee bars 8am/9am to late afternoon/early evening
Bars and pubs 4pm until late; limited menu in the evening (usually until 10pm)
Restaurants Noon to 2.30pm and 6pm/7pm until 10pm

Going Out

Club scene Large nightclubs are a dying breed in Belgium, but Brussels keeps the flame alive with the legendary **Fuse** (p124) among others. Bruges is quieter, with revelry usually unfolding in bars and cafes around Eiermarkt.

Party time Although midnight is fine, the party really kicks off around 1am. In bars, the vibe is getting hot around 10pm.

Door policy It depends on the club – some are more selective than others, often denying entry to solo males or all-male groups. Dress well, stay relaxed, wear a smile and you'll usually get in without trouble.

Cover charge Admission is typically around €20, or as low as €10 if bought early. There's also the Brussels Volume Pass: granting you access to two clubs in one night (€29) or unlimited entry for 48 hours (€48), plus free entry to select museums and the Atomium.

HOW MUCH FOR A

Pils from tap (25cl) €3.20–3.50

Bottle of craft beer €5.50

Glass of wine €5–7

Cocktail €10–15

Dry sausage/cheese cubes €2.50/6

Cone of frites €4

Bicky burger €3.50–4.50

Liège waffle €2.50–3

LGBTIQ+ Travellers

Belgium warmly welcomes LGBTIQ+ travellers with lively queer scenes, especially in major cities, though occasional prejudice may still be encountered.

Gaybourhoods

Centred around the Plattesteen and rue du Charbon, Brussels' **Rainbow Village** grew organically as gay men embraced visibility and safe spaces. Today, it's a lively LGBTIQ+ hotspot with bars (cruising or not), drag shows, cabarets and queer-centred shopping. At its heart is the Rainbow House, a community centre offering support and social activities for all.

While Bruges is generally a welcoming and inclusive place for travellers, it is a small city and lacks a large LGBTIQ+ scene. However, in mid-June the city holds the **Bruges Pride Parade** while **Vrijplaats Brugge** serves as the community's centre.

Best LGBTIQ+ Spots

La Démence Once a month at Fuse, the largest gay men's club night.

Chez Maman Legendary drag show cabaret in Brussels.

The Crazy Circle Brussels' relaxed lesbian, feminist and queer bar.

Qbar Bruges' queer community gathering place.

NITO/SHUTTERSTOCK

BRUSSELS PRIDE

Belgium's biggest Pride celebration draws a crowd of 150,000+ each May, with a week of events building to the fabulously extravagant Saturday march. Come one, come all!

LGBTIQ+ TOURS

L-tour shows you the city of Brussels through a queer lens during Pride Week and other events.

Resources

● **Rainbowhouse** (Brussels) Provides information, assistance, a meeting spot and a safe place for the LGBTIQ+ community. *rainbowhouse.be* ● **Cavaria** The umbrella organisation federating Rainbow Houses and associations, in Flanders. *cavaria.be* ● **BrUIT** Bruges association organising events for the community in the area. *facebook .com/bruit.brugge*

Health & Safe Travel

Brussels and especially Bruges are pretty safe for visitors but as anywhere, keep an eye open.

TAP WATER

Tap water is perfectly safe in Belgium but locals tend to buy bottled water as it 'tastes better' according to many. Note that very few restaurants offer free water, so you'll have to order a bottle with your meal.

Parapharmacy vs Pharmacy

In recent years, parapharmacies (*parapharmacies/parafarmacieën*) have multiplied, selling everything from hair products to first-aid kits. Don't expect over-the-counter medicines here: at most, you'll get a herbal syrup for a mild cough. For anything else, even minor ailments, head to a *pharmacie/apotheek*. Our tip? Pack basic first-aid supplies. After hours, on-call pharmacies are posted on doors or call +32 903 99 000.

Transport

Driving, riding or cycling while intoxicated is punishable by a fine, as is fare dodging.

Health Insurance

Purchasing travel insurance is strongly recommended, especially for non-EU residents. EU citizens (including Iceland, Liechtenstein, Norway and Switzerland) should carry the free European Health Insurance Card (EHIC) for local-rate medical care. UK residents should use the UK Global Health Insurance Card (GHIC), which replaces the EHIC and provides similar coverage across most European countries.

— **PETTY CRIMES** —

Pickpocketing and bag-snatching does happen. Keep your wits about you, especially at train stations (particularly in Brussels) and while on public transportation.

QUICK INFO

Security
Renting a bike? Lock it or park it in a box when not in use.

Alcohol
The blood alcohol limit while driving is 0.5g/l.

Cannabis
Possession is decriminalised: over-18s may carry up to 3g for personal use.

149

Responsible Travel

Follow these tips to leave a lighter footprint, support local businesses and have a positive impact on communities.

Recycling Glass Bottles

In Belgium, many beer bottles come with a *'consigne/statiegeld'*, a deposit you pay when purchasing and get back upon returning the empty bottles to shops or supermarkets. These are then washed and reused. If a bottle isn't *consignée* (look for the logo) or if a shop cannot accept it, don't worry, you can still recycle it by dropping it at the numerous glass collection points in town.

Train Travel

Belgium is blessed with extensive **railway networks** *(belgiantrain.be)* connecting its cities, towns and neighbouring countries, making travelling by train a breeze. And there's no need to buy tickets in advance.

OUR PICK

Good Food

The **Good Food** *(goodfood.brussels)* label honours Brussels restaurants using local, seasonal produce, promoting ecofriendly practices, protein alternatives and waste reduction.

Ride a Bike

Brussels and compact Bruges are great for cycling. Brussels has around 513km of cycling paths, allowing cyclists to bike safely. Bike rentals abound in both cities but **Blue Bikes** *(blue-bike.be)*, located at Bruges and Bruxelles-Central train stations, are convenient options. **Villo** *(villo.be)* is Brussels' bike-sharing service.

To plan your itinerary in Brussels go to routeplanner.bike.brussels; find information about biking in Bruges at visitbruges.be/en/things-to-do/sightseeing/cycling.

Resources

● **visit.brussels/en/visitors/what-to-do/sustainable-brussels** Visit Brussels in a responsible way. ● **visitbruges.be/en/things-to-do/about-bruges/sustainable-tourism** Bruges' sustainable list. ● **visit.brussels/en/visitors/plan-your-trip/greeters** Discover Brussels with a local greeter.

—— **FOOD WITH A PURPOSE** ——

Profits from Elliott Van de Velde's restaurant **Entropy** (p103) are used to support his Hearth Project's initiatives against food waste and social inequality.

Conscious Shopping

Think 'recycling' and 'shopping' and vintage stores probably come to mind. Brussels is full of them! Find unique pieces at **Bernard Gavilan** (p125), **Foxhole** (p125) or, for creators, **Isabelle Bajart** (p105). You can also shop for locally made souvenirs at **Manneke** (p105), **D'EN Belge** (p105) or **Jinzu** (p124) ceramics.

The **Handmade in Brugge** initiative supports local craftspeople and artisans. Pick up the booklet from the tourist board, or visit the showcase **Sashuis** (p76) store near the Begijnhof.

LOW EMISSION ZONES

Bringing your own car? Brussels has established Low Emission Zones, restricting older and more polluting vehicles from entering. Scan the QR code to apply for the mandatory pass.

Climate Change & Travel

It's impossible to ignore the impact we have when travelling; Lonely Planet urges all travellers to engage with their travel carbon footprint, which will mainly come from air travel. While there often isn't an alternative, travellers can look to minimise the number of flights they take, opt for newer aircraft and use cleaner ground transport, such as trains. One proposed solution – purchasing carbon offsets – unfortunately does not cancel out the impact of individual flights. While most destinations will depend on air travel for the foreseeable future, for now, pursuing ground-based travel where possible is the best course of action.

The **UN Carbon Offset Calculator** shows how flying impacts a household's emissions

The **ICAO's carbon emissions calculator** allows visitors to analyse the CO_2 generated by point-to-point journeys

Accessible Travel

Public Transport

Belgian railways *(belgiantrain.be/en/travel-info/ prepare-for-your-journey/assistance-reduced-mobility)* offers free assistance for mobility impaired passengers. Book online, or three hours ahead at major stations. Brussels **metros** *(www.stib-mivb.be/travel/prm/ access-to-stops-stations-and-vehicles)* have Braille signs, tactile tiles and lifts with assistance. Most trams and buses in both cities are now accessible.

Museum Access

Museums are widely accessible to wheelchairs (although some rooms might not be). Unfortunately, Bruges' Belfry and Gruuthusemuseum are not.

Take a View

Mobility-impaired visitors can enjoy Bruges' skyline from the top floor of the **Concertgebouw** (p72). A ticket for the Concertgebouw Circuit grants lift access, city views, and exhibitions inside.

ACCOMMODATION

Large hotels and well-established brands have accessible rooms available. For smaller hotels, historic buildings, B&Bs and short-term rentals, this is often not the case. Make sure to check in advance.

COBBLESTONE STREETS

Cobblestone streets, one thing both cities have in common, can be challenging for wheelchair users, as well as the visually impaired and anyone with balance/mobility challenges, due to their uneven surfaces.

OUR PICK

Brussels' **Musées Royaux des Beaux-Arts** (p110) provide facilities for visually and hearing-impaired visitors, while the **Musée Magritte** (p112) lends visio-guides and audio-description guides (€4).

Most museums in Brussels and Bruges provide free entry for disabled visitors or carers (a European Disability Card may be required). Online ticketing systems show availability, allowing you to choose quieter time slots.

For neurodivergent visitors, the **Museum Sint-Janshospitaal** (p63), **Volkskunde-museum** (p49) and **Gruuthusemuseum** (p66) provide free sensory kits to reduce or stimulate sensory inputs.

Resources

● **visitbruges.be/en/plan-your-visit/accessibility** Information and brochure for an accessible Bruges. ● **visit.brussels/en/visitors/plan-your-trip/practical-info/ accessibility** Visiting Brussels is for everyone.

Nuts & Bolts

Opening Hours

Note that the following hours may vary.

Banks 9am–4pm or 5pm

Bars 5pm or 6pm–midnight or 1am

Cafes 8am–8pm

Clubs 10pm–3am or 6am

Post offices 9am–5pm (with possible noon break between 12.30pm and 1.30pm)

Restaurants noon–2pm and 6pm–10pm

Shopping malls 9am or 10am–7pm

Shops 10am–6pm (with a possible lunch break)

Supermarkets 8am–8pm

Ouvert/Open
Open
Fermé/Gesloten
Closed

QUICK INFO

Time zone Central European Time (GMT/UTC +1 in winter/ +2 in summer)

City codes +02 (Brussels); +050 (Bruges)

Emergency number 112

Population 1,255,795 (Brussels); 119,765 (Bruges)

ELECTRICITY
230V/50Hz

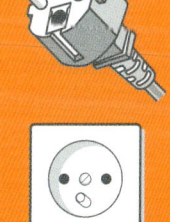

Type E
220V/50Hz

Public Holidays

Shops and services will likely be closed on the following dates.

New Year's Day
1 January

Easter Monday
March/April

Labour Day
1 May

Ascension Day
May

Whit Monday
May/June

National Day
21 July

Assumption Day
15 August

All Saints' Day
1 November

Armistice Day
11 November

Christmas Day
25 December

Smoking

Smoking and vaping are strictly prohibited indoors (in restaurants, offices, public buildings such as airports), except in designated areas and on outdoor station platforms. Smoking is still allowed on open terraces, but the law may change soon.

Languages

French/Dutch Basics

Hello.
Bonjour. / Dag.
bon·zhoor / dakh

Goodbye.
Au revoir. / Dag.
o·rer·vwa / dakh

Yes.
Oui. / Ja. *wee / yaa*

No.
Non. / Nee. *non / ney*

Please.
S'il vous plaît. / Alstublieft. *seel voo play / al·stew·bleeft*

Thank you.
Merci. / Dank u.
mair·see / dangk ew

Excuse me.
Excusez-moi. / Excuseer mij.
ek·skew·zay·mwa / eks·kew·zeyr mey

💬 Fast Phrases

How are you?
Comment allez-vous? / Hoe gaat het met u?
ko·mon ta·lay·voo / hoo khaat huht met ew

Fine.
Bien. / Goed. *byun / khoot*

Do you speak English?
Parlez-vous anglais? / Spreekt u Engels?
par·lay·voo ong·glay / spreykt ew eng·uhls

I don't understand.
Je ne comprends pas. / Ik begrijp het niet. *zher ner kom·pron pa / ik buh·khreyp huht neet*

How much is it?
C'est combien? / Hoeveel kost het? *say kom·byun / hoo·veyl kost huht*

I'd like the bill, please.
Je voudrais l'addition, s'il vous plaît. / Ik wil graag de rekening, alstublieft. *zher voo·dray la·dee·syon seel voo play / ik wil khraakh duh rey·kuh·ning al·stew·bleeft*

Where are the toilets?
Où sont les toilettes? / Waar zijn de toiletten? *oo son lay twa·let/waar zeyn duh twa·le·tuhn*

Where's the...?
Où est ...? / Waar is ...? *oo ay ... / waar is*

Help!
Au secours! / Help! *o skoor / help*

Numbers

 un / één
un / eyn

 deux / twee
der / twey

 trois / drie
trwa / dree

 quatre / vier
ka·tre / veer

 cinq / vijf
sungk / veyf

Good to Know

Belgium is split into Dutch-speaking Flanders (Vlaanderen in Dutch) and French-speaking Wallonia (la Wallonie in French), as well as a small German-speaking region.

Bruges is Flemish and therefore Dutch-speaking. Brussels is officially bilingual, though French has long been the city's dominant language.

Most of the sounds used in French and Dutch can be found in English. If you read our pronunciation guides below as if they were English, you'll be understood just fine.

To enhance your trip with a phrasebook, visit **shop. lonelyplanet.com**.

TABLE ETIQUETTE

The menu, please.
La carte, s'il vous plaît. / Een menu, alstublieft. *la·dee·syon seel voo play / uhn me·new al·stew·bleeft*

Delicious!
Délicieux! / Heerlijk! *day·lee·syer / heyr·luhk*

Cheers!
Santé! / Proost! *son·tay / prohst*

Signs

Entrée/Ingang Entrance
Sortie/Uitgang Exit
Ouvert/Open Open
Fermé/Gesloten Closed
Interdit/Verboden Prohibited
Pousser/Duwen Push
Tirer/Trekken Pull
Toilettes/Toiletten Toilets
Femmes/Dames Women
Hommes/Heren Men

Listen For

Your passport/visa, please.
Votre passeport/visa, s'il vous plaît. / Uw paspoort/visum, alstublieft. *vo·trer pas·por/vee·za seel voo play / ew pas·pohrt/vee·zum al·stew·bleeft*

——— SLANG TO LISTEN OUT FOR ———

Cool! **Génial! / Leuk!** *zhay·nyal / leuk*

Sure. **D'accord. / Natuurlijk.** *da·kor / na·tewr·luhk*

No problem. **Pas de soucis. / Geen probleem.** *pa der soo·see / kheyn proh·bleym*

No way! **Pas question! / Geen sprake van!** *pa kay·styon / kheyn spraa·kuh van*

Just joking! **Je plaisante! / Grapje!** *zher play·zont / khrap·yuh*

6	**7**	**8**	**9**	**10**
six / zes *sees / zes*	**sept / zeven** *set / zey·vuhn*	**huit / acht** *weet / akht*	**neuf / negen** *nerf / ney·khuhn*	**dix / tien** *dees / teen*

Index

Sights p000   Map pages p000

See also separate subindexes for:
- **Eating p158**
- **Drinking p159**
- **Shopping p159**

Eating

Drinking

Shopping

Send Us Your Feedback

We love to hear from travellers – your comments help make our books better. We read every word, and we guarantee that your feedback goes straight to the authors. Visit lonelyplanet.com/contact to submit your updates and suggestions.

Note: We may edit, reproduce and incorporate your comments in Lonely Planet products such as guidebooks, websites and digital products, so let us know if you are happy to have your name acknowledged. For a copy of our privacy policy visit lonelyplanet.com/legal.

Acknowledgements

Cover photograph: Boat on canal in Bruges (p33). Ludwig WALLENDORFF/REA/Redux

Back photograph: Maison du Roi (p86), Brussels. Werner Lerooy/Shutterstock

THIS BOOK

The 7th edition of Lonely Planet's *Pocket Bruges & Brussels* guidebook was researched and written by Mélissa Monaco and Helena Smith, who also wrote the previous edition. This guidebook was produced by the following:

Destination Editor
Annemarie McCarthy

Coordinating Editor
Tasmin Waby

Cartographer
David Connolly

Production Editor
Will Allen

Image Editor Rita Harper

Assisting Editors
Janet Austin, Kellie Langdon, Jenna Myers, Charlotte Orr

Cover Researcher
Kat Marsh

Thanks to
Fergal Condon, Gwen Cotter, Sandie Kestell, Darren O'Connell, Saralinda Turner

Although the authors and Lonely Planet have taken all reasonable care in preparing this book, we make no warranty about the accuracy or completeness of its content and, to the maximum extent permitted, disclaim all liability arising from its use.

Published by Lonely Planet Global Limited
CRN 554153
7th edition – June 2026
ISBN 978 1 83869 878 2
© Lonely Planet 2026
10 9 8 7 6 5 4 3 2 1
Printed in China